Romantic Relationships in Islam

Romantic Relationships in Islam

✦

Understanding how Love functions within Islam

Muhammed Amin Ibrahim

iUniverse, Inc.

New York Lincoln Shanghai

Romantic Relationships in Islam
Understanding how Love functions within Islam

iUniverse, Inc.

For information address:
iUniverse, Inc.
2021 Pine Lake Road, Suite 100
Lincoln, NE 68512
www.iuniverse.com

ISBN: 0-595-32886-5 (pbk)
ISBN: 0-595-66702-3 (cloth)

Printed in the United States of America

Dedicated to all the women and men around the world craving for true love

Contents

In the Name of God, the Compassionate, the Merciful

INTRODUCTION

To the extent that most people are aware of Islam, their views are strongly influenced by such dramatic events as the September 11 terrorist attacks in New York and Washington; the war in Afghanistan; events in Iraq; the threatening pronouncements of Osama Bin Laden and his most trusted lieutenant—Ayman Al-Zawahiri; the Bali bombings in Indonesia; activities of Muslim separatists in the Philippines; and the global war against terror. To focus solely on these events, however significant, perpetuates several unfortunate misperceptions about Islam. Recognizing the need to step beyond these stereotypes and headlines, the purpose of this book is to explore romantic relationships between the opposite sex from an Islamic viewpoint. There is a general feeling of malaise today in our world, uneasy as it is, with the prevalence of ever-rising divorce rates, sexual infidelity (even at the highest levels), and a concomitant sexually transmitted disease—HIV/AIDS. The iconoclastic attitude toward the institution of marriage is widespread among today's youth—an indicator that, the word "love" has lost it's meaning and significance. This writer intends to re-examine the concept of love and romance in Islam—a religion that has been, and is still widely misunderstood.

Writing about how love functions within the Islamic religion is a field no writer could claim originality about. A huge mass of facts has already been collected over a 1500 year period by scholars and researchers of all hues and shades, and among them non-Muslim polemicists concerning family life in Islam. It is from this ocean of information that this writer has to choose how to go about explaining how love functions within Islam. All that he intends to do is to arrange the facts in a certain order according to what he wishes to substantiate. The purpose of this book is simple. It is to provide a quick and authentic account of the relationship between love and sex from an Islamic viewpoint. This writer makes no attempt to burden the reader with lengthy details or discourse. While avoiding the temptation of any pedantic or daunting display of notes and references, this writer do provide some documentation to lead the inquisitive reader to some original sources.

Without breaking his links with the original sources, the writer makes use of his long experience as an Arabic and Islamic teacher in Ghana and Nigeria, and his long experience in dealing with romantic affairs as a student in Ghana and as a religious teacher in Nigeria before leaving for the Middle East and the Far East for further studies. One other useful aspect of this book is it's effort, within it's small scope to bridge the gap between love and marriage, true and fake love—emphasizing that true love should inevitable lead to marriage. This book's major shortcoming may be that those comfortably positioned on one side of the bridge may be unwilling to cross it. The first chapter of this book examines the relationship between love and sex. It argues that love does not mean sex, and vice-versa. The second chapter focuses on the general topic of love, and attempts to explain it's meaning from an Islamic point of view.

The third chapter argues that God is the source of all love. It establishes the authenticity of the Arabic Qur'an as revealed to the Prophet of Islam, Muhammad (peace be upon him). The fourth and fifth chapters discuss the journey lovers should take before reaching the ultimate goal: marriage. The fourth specifically deals with the preparations needed to be done before undertaking this journey. The fifth then discusses what is to be done at the end of this journey. The sixth chapter discusses what is to be done after the consummation of marriage, and/or how to create good times for lovers and keep the good times rolling. The seventh chapter re-examines the state of love in our patriarchal world, arguing that true and genuine love is fast disappearing.

Science and reason may have failed, when it comes to dealing with problems of the human heart. Today, we are witnessing a new revolution that will shape the knowledge society of the 21st Century—The Digital Revolution—driven by the accelerating convergence of the Internet, broadcast media and Information and Communication Technologies (ICT). This revolution affects all aspects of our life-styles, the way we learn, work and communicate with each other; but will it be able to keep marriages intact; insure loyalty between married couples; put a stop to child prostitution and pornography; end violence against women once and for all? In short will it make the world a better and safer place to conduct faithful relationships? The answer to these questions are being blown by strong typhoon winds across the Pacific Ocean that can't even be detected by the world's most powerful spy satellites!

Although it is not every woman or man's intention to get married or have a baby, this is a woman doctor who cries out saying: "Take away my certificate and give me a husband." Let us read what that poor doctor writes in her own words: "Every morning at 7am, I shed tears behind the chauffeur who drives me in my car to the medical clinic, 'prison cell' or 'grave'. She went on saying: "Every time I reached my destination, I found women and children waiting for me. They looked at me with admiration and regarded my white coat as if it were luxurious clothes made of Persian silk. Yet it was in my view—the 'mourner's clothes'. And every time I reached my clinic, I fixed the stethoscope, as if it were a hangman's rope tied around my neck."

She continues, "Now I'm in my thirties and I'm very pessimistic about the future." Then she cries out! "Take away my certificate, my coats and my money, and let me hear the word MUM." Then she writes a few lines describing her inner feelings: "People would call me a doctor, but what benefit do I get from hearing it. So tell those who considered me as a good example that, now I'm to be pitied. All I want and hope for is to have my own child to hug and caress. But can I buy it with all my money?"[1]

Add to that a somber Princess Diana—the People's Princess—telling of a lonely and desperate existence in her early-married life to the Prince of Wales, Prince Charles. This is what Diana had to say: "My husband made me feel so inadequate in every possible way," she told her biographer Andrew Morton. "Every time, I tried to come up for air, he pushed me down again." Princess Diana also talks about her several suicide attempts: "I threw myself down the stairs bearing in mind I was carrying a child," she said, describing one incident. "Queen (Elizabeth) comes out, absolutely horrified, shaking she's so frightened…and Charles went out riding."[2] The Princess died at age 36 in a 1997 auto accident in Paris. In Diana's case she was unhappy because her marriage could be said to have been devoid of compassion and affection. "I never wanted a divorce and always dreamt of a happy marriage with loving support from Charles." She wrote, according to her former butler and confidant Paul Burrell. "A part of me would always love Charles,"[3] she added.

---

1. Ghalib Ahmad Masri and Nathif Jami Adam, *The Way To happiness* (Riyadh: The Cooperative Office for Call and Guidance, under the Supervision of the Presidency for Islamic Research, Ifta and Propagation, n.d.), 48-49.
2. *MSNBC*, "In tapes, Diana speaks of marriage woes," [news on-line]; available from http://www.msnbc.msn.com/id/4456925/; Internet; accessed 6 March 2004, p.1 of 4.

People have grown so busy that personal relationships are impoverished. Friendships are harder to maintain. Families are shrinking, and not only through divorce. People in developed countries are now having fewer children, and the elderly are not often cared for at home. Despite globalization, communities are growing smaller and more private as people (and even) nations sort themselves into haves and have-nots. Despite all these, one is apt to hear aphorisms like: "A friend in need is a friend indeed; tell me your friend and I will tell you his character; there is no better mirror than an old friend; you may find your best friend or your worst enemy in your self, etc." These aphorisms may make you yawn, but they are sometimes the most effective way to characterize or sum up personal relationships.

Although human relationships have been categorized into many types, relationships with the opposite sex have been the most common in all cultures under the sun. This relationship could just be a platonic one; it could also be a romantic one; however, the romantic one could be the *sweetest*. As far as romantic relationships are concerned, it's the same in the East and in the West. Differences, however, would not fail to exist with respect to it's longevity, closeness and intensity. The word "love" or "lover" is used so freely nowadays that it may not necessarily indicate the dichotomy between an amorous relationship, whereby one partner is usually considered only as a "usable and expendable commodity", and an intimate companionship, whereby the ultimate goal is matrimony. Some men like to boast about their priapic conquests. Some sailors are reputedly famous for their priapic episodes ashore (a girl in every port).

Although it is a fact that most teachings of Islam concerning love, sex and marriage are not strictly adhered to, by many of today's Muslims, such deviations should not be unfairly exaggerated or superficially taken by some writers to represent the teachings of Islam to a lay reader. These writers should take the extra mile of making original and unbiased study of the authentic sources of these teachings.

Muhammed Amin Ibrahim

Taipei, April 2004

---

3.   Burrell said Diana sent him a handwritten note on August 26, 1996, the day her divorce from Charles was finalized.

1

LOVE AND SEX: COINJOINED TWINS?

Matters that touch "on the area below the waist" as Japanese say, had better be left unsaid and so on. However, people obsessed by sexuality often complain that sex is a "perverse little devil," and that the minute you ignore it, it has a serious temper tantrum and tries every trick in the book to get your attention; unless of course, according to them, you suffer from a sex sickness—or that you are sick of sex. These afflictions, according to them, come in different forms. In any case, sexual stirrings seem to have an inordinate influence over our lives—not necessarily in the expression of the act it's self, but in the yearning, scheming, talking about, and even the ruing of it. Yet, despite all this attention, the forces that drive us sexually remain among the baffling aspects of our lives. Why, in the midst of a perfectly happy and satisfying relationship, do we sometimes get an incredibly strong urge to be unfaithful?[1] There is no need to over state the strong relationship between love and sex as this book is neither intended to be a book on psychology, evolutionary biology or sociology.

The Natural Bond

Let's open the Book of God—The Holy Qur'an and read the following verse:

> "Fair in the eyes of men
>
> Is the love of things they covet:
>
> Women and sons;
>
> Heaped-up hoards

---

1.   Robin Baker, *Sperm Wars: The Science of Sex,* (New York: Basic Books, 1996), xiii.

> Of gold and silver; horse
> Branded (for blood and excellence);
> And (wealth of) cattle
> And well-tilled land.
> Such are the possessions
> Of this world's life;
> But with Allah
> Is the best of the goals
> (To return to)."[2]

The pleasures of this life are first enumerated: Women for love; sons for strength and pride; hoarded riches, that procure all luxuries; the best and finest pedigree of horses; cattle, the measure of wealth in the ancient world (and in some parts of Africa until date); as well as the means and symbols of good farming in the modern world; and broad acres of well-tilled land. By analogy, we may include, for our electronic age, Super Computers, Spy Satellites, B-52 Bombers, Bunker Busters, Nuclear Submarines, Aircraft Carriers, Inter-Continental Ballistic Missiles (ICBMs), Nuclear Arsenal, Weapons of Mass Destruction (WMD), and so on. Finally, and heaped-up hoards of gold and silver.

What we notice immediately after reading this verse is the relationship that occurs between a man and a woman. That relationship is bonded together by love. God has preceded all other things that are coveted by men in this life with the love of women (that appeals to men most). We also realize from this verse that the love that occurs actually has to occur between a man and a woman—not between a man and another man. God has even preceded the love for sons with the love of women; the love of wealth; and all that men regard as sources of power that they want to take exclusive possession of. From this verse, we notice the strong relationship between love and sexual instincts. And, since men and women belong to the same species, the satisfaction of a sexual instinct can only be realized when both sexes are present, and in the mood. At this point, both become attracted to each other, then they both fall in love. This love (whether a fake or a true one), engenders a sexual arousal that begins to behave like that "naughty child" who wouldn't let it's parents go to sleep, because it can't fall asleep too. Both partners will be expected to appease this "child'" to fall asleep. Now, a right approach must be taken in the form of caressing, rocking or feeding it with breast

---

2.   Qur'an, 3:14.

milk. All these measures could fail if done carelessly. Indeed it could even lead to the direct opposite—the "child" becoming more aggressive.

Whether or not the "child" would finally be appeased depends upon the type of antidote administered. The desired objective could be either to tame this child just for one night or tame it for a much longer period. In either case, it will depend upon how the "parents" handle that situation. This analogy applies to true love; that leads to a long and enduring sexual relationship; and fake love that leads to say—a one-night stand—after which both partners disappear. There are millions of men and women today who only have sex partners, and not lovers. How do we say of a man, who would say to a woman "I love you", would be ready to "shack up" with her, but would not contemplate marriage—even if she remains the only woman on earth? The same could be said of a woman too. To be sure, the meaning of "I love you" has turned into "I need you". In other words, "I love you" has acquired the ostensible meaning of "I need you to satisfy my sexual cravings". From an Islamic point of view, the media has seriously ruptured the meaning of love. Instead of calling them sex partners, the media depict them as lovers! It's all right to have a sex partner, if one wishes to do so. But is it not also instructive to call a spade a spade?

The Distortion of the Natural Bond

In order to demonstrate how the meaning of love has been distorted over a very long period of time, I would like to allude to certain incidents in the past. And although, some may appear offensive to the reader, for the purpose of illustration, it would still be worthwhile to mention them. As a secondary school student growing up in Ghana, I had a friend who happened to be my senior. I will call him Wumbee (not his real name). Wumbee was a real womanizer who admitted to me that fornication was in his blood, and for that reason, he could not resist it. Wumbee said in his quest to satisfy himself sexually, the looks of a woman bothered him not. According to him, even if a woman had very bad looks so much so that he could not stand her, he wouldn't mind using a piece of cloth to cover her face during sexual intercourse—his main goal was to derive satisfaction—and that he wouldn't allow a woman's bad looks be a deterrent. There may be several Wumbees hiding in all the four corners of the globe. In this our modern world, why should women in some parts of the world still be considered as "usable and expendable commodities"? Has the true meaning of love disappeared from our classrooms?

There was another guy, I will call him Dawuni, (not his real name). He was not different from Wumbee. He was equally lecherous like him. However, he had a different method. He once showed me a book (he called it his register). This 'register' contained names of his girl friends around the country. It also documented the number of times he has slept with each of them. If my memory still serves me right, I counted about 15 unfortunate girls in his so-called register. As I browsed through it, I realized he had marked 15 beside the name of a particular girl. "What did the number 15 mean?" I asked Dawuni. He said it meant he has slept with that particular girl 15 times. There were figures beside the names of all those young girls in this 'register'. What was even so provocative was the fact that, he wrote these words boldly on the entrance leading to his bedroom: "The Office of Sex Administration." Dawuni could not be easily persuaded to give up his sexual adventures. After all, who complains of being a youth during which time the exhilaration of life is felt in the very bones?

In the mid 1990s, during my student days in Taipei, I used to go and practice soccer during the week-ends at the National Taiwan University's football field with other foreigners including Chinese. Coming from a soccer-loving country like Ghana, where soccer is almost a religion, I had developed considerable interest in the game since youth. It was during this period that I became acquainted with Domingo (not his real name) from a Spanish-speaking Central American nation.[3] It was our mutual love for soccer that brought us so close. Domingo had been in Taiwan to study Chinese and had barely lived in Taiwan for six months. However, he was fond of bragging about his priapic episodes—he once told me he had already had sex with 19 different girls since his arrival in Taipei six months earlier. This was a young man in his early twenties. Domingo would not disclose to me how he managed to prey on these unsuspecting Chinese girls. And, although he spoke little Chinese, he pronounced the sentence *Wo ai ni* (I love you) in Chinese, with great accuracy. Was this the magic expression he used on his prey? I have yet to find an answer.

A Taipei newspaper reported in 1999, that twenty-two percent of Taipei's teen-agers have had sexual relations and that 15 percent of those were between the ages of 13 and 15, citing a survey released by the Travel and Medicine Association. According to the report, among a total of 417 adolescents aged between 12 and 19 polled by the association, 91 claimed to have had intimate relations with others, and 28 said their first sexual experience had taken place during a recent

3.   Name of country deliberately withheld by author. It's a diplomatic ally of Taiwan, which has few such countries that recognize it.

summer vacation. Over 70 percent of those polled said they have been exposed to pornographic books, videotapes, CD-ROMs, and other media containing sexual material. Several male respondents said they had erotic thoughts every five to ten minutes and one claimed to have had sexual relations seven times within a week with as many different girls. Most female respondents said they were CON-FUSED AT TELLING LOVE FROM SEX, and many said they worried about being pregnant or infected with venereal diseases from having intercourse. According to the report, the telephone survey was conducted on 182 girls and 235 boys between June 28 to August 12, 1999.

In the same report, the newspaper indicated that the Taipei Medical College (now Taipei Medical University) held a news conference and invited a number of teens to tell their own opinion about sex. "Some of my classmates have sex two or three times a day, and it's not surprising that they do it more than ten times a week." Said a 19 year-old male college student. "Boys like to brag about how many girls they've 'engaged' while chatting with each other," he added. "There is nothing wrong with having sex. The point is that you should always wear a con-dom to avoid possible consequences," said Ah yuan, another college student. Ah yuan said that he would not mind if his girl friend had a one-night stand with someone else, but he would not do it himself because he feels it's "dirty." Ah yuan suggested school authorities set up automated condom dispensers on cam-pus.[4]

In her letter to an advice column, one American woman had this to say about her 13 year-old daughter: "I am a 29 year-old single mother of a 13 year-old daughter. When people do the math, It's clear that I myself was a teen at the time of her birth. Now that my daughter is a teen, I constantly worry about her having sex and getting pregnant. I have conversations with her periodically about safe sex and abstinence, and I know she doesn't want to hear about it, but I still continue to stress the issue. She tells me she isn't having sex and isn't interested in boys right now. Up until recently, I had no reason to disbelieve her. However, one day, my daughter was talking on the phone, and I just felt the need to pick up the phone and eavesdrop. She was talking to a boy."

The writer continued: "I know this boy's family, so I figured it wouldn't be too bad. I was wrong. He was talking about getting an apartment with her and going out to dinner and then coming home to their apartment and putting rose petals on the bed. He was also asking her how many kids she would like to have. My daughter responded by telling him that she didn't know because she is still set

---

4.   *China Post* (Taipei), 27 August 1999.

on going to school to be a doctor after she graduates from college. After this, he tells her that she won't have to worry about going to college because he will go for the both of them so she can stay at home and be a housewife. He then goes on about how his birthday is coming, and he would like her to have sex with him as a present. She then said she really doesn't want to talk about sex. When I asked her later who was on the phone, She said it was her cousin. I need help—Worried Mom."[5]

Now, how many couples do go out to dinner, return to their apartment, and scatter rose petals on the bed? This, undoubtedly, is a young boy's idea of sex. In his seduction spiel, the young boy goes as far as promising his lover that he would go to college for the both of them! One might be compelled to ask, Is there a WALL or should there be a WALL between LOVE and SEX? If there is any, or if there should be, how thick and tall should it be? For this writer, there is only a very thin WALL between love and sex, and that is the CONDOM. If we, as human beings are unable to answer such questions honestly, then how can we claim to be better than animals? Here and there, we find a 13 year-old being asked to 'dole out' sex as a birthday present to her "lover", and a group of girls not being able to DIFFERENTIATE between LOVE and SEX. This writer is among the very few in the world who believe that Love Education should be used as a substitute for Sex Education. Whether one is an atheist, a Buddhist; a Christian; a Hindu, belongs to Islam; a Jew; believes in Shintoism; a Taoist; or a Zoroastrian, we all have the responsibility to re-discover the meaning of love, re-package it, and market it skillfully to coming generations. There is a movement among the unmarried public called "the new celibacy," that stresses companionship without sex. One gets the feeling these movements will be short-lived especially if they are devoid of divine guidance.

Nowadays, many teens also wonder if "abstinence-only" sex education is realistic. A high school student counts on her fingers as she poses a question to a couple of high school classmates: "How many girls in our class were pregnant before our junior year?" the 18-year-old senior asks. They came out with about five out of seventy-five girls. It's an illustration, they say of teenage life in America. At a time when sexually transmitted diseases present serious health risks to young people, current US President Bush has suggested doubling federal funding for "abstinence-only" sex education. But many teens see that approach as unrealistic.[6] "No matter what adults say, some kids are going to have sex anyway," The high school

5.   *China Post* (Taipei), 23 April 2004.
6.   *Taiwan News* (Taipei), 16 March 2004.

students concluded. Earlier this year, in the US State of Minnesota, health officials released an independent evaluation of an abstinence-only pilot program called Education Now and Babies Later—one of the first evaluations of any program of it's kind. The survey found that sexual activity has doubled among junior high school students who took part in it.

Evaluators recommended broadening the program to include more information about contraception. But abstinence proponents questioned the study's validity and said that the program would have been more successful if it suggested teens waited until marriage to have sex, rather than just until they were older. "Waiting until marriage," says a 16 year-old high school student, "I think, is a good idea." She had learned about sexually transmitted diseases during a recent health class and hearing that information helped reinforce her decision to wait for sex. "You realize how dangerous it can be," she said. However, another 18 year-old rolls her eyes at the thought of waiting until marriage. "I'm not going to say 'no' if I'm dating someone for a long time," she says. To her, having sex is a personal decision, one that should be made carefully and with direct, simple information about reliable birth control. That information she says, would be more helpful to her and her peers than being told 'just to say no'—or, as she did for one class, taking a "pretend baby" home and caring for it over a weekend to learn the responsibilities of parenthood.

"It wasn't really that hard. I even took by 'baby' to the movies with a couple of friends," she says, noting that her parent's own situation did much more to make her want to avoid pregnancy early in life. "My Mom had four kids by age 25," she says. "It wasn't easy." Her classmate and fellow senior, says her parents have influenced her ideas about sex, too—but in a different way, because she knows they'd be disappointed if she were to get pregnant before she was married. "I would feel terrible because my parents have such a high regard and respect for me," "I would feel like I let them down."[7] Reading between the lines, one realizes that the line between love and sex has become blurred as far as 21st Century love is concerned. Should every love affair lead to sex? From the above, one also realizes that the "World of Sex" belongs to the man. It seems it has always been the man who is apt to demand for sex from his partner, and if she obliges, she might end up finding her self at the short end of the stick—an unwanted pregnancy that might have to be aborted!

In 1970, a survey of more than 3000 adults entitled "Sex and Morality was conducted in the U.S. At that time, it was the only survey of sex and morality in

---

7.   *Ibid.*

a representative sample of the U.S. population before the spread of AIDS. The Kinsey institute sex survey was aimed at helping researchers understand how AIDS was spread. "A majority disapproved of homosexuality, prostitution, extra-marital sex," the authors of the survey wrote. Furthermore, they said, "a majority of Americans are 'moral absolutists' in that they see these behaviors as always wrong." Extramarital sex was described as "always wrong" or "almost always wrong" by 87 percent of the respondents. Homosexual relations among people who don't love each other were described the same way by 88 percent of the respondents. Even among individuals who loved each other, homosexual sex was disapproved by 79 percent of the respondents. Eighty-two percent disapproved of teen-age girls having premarital sex; 73 percent disapprove of teen-age boys hav-ing premarital sex; 70 percent disapproved of adult premarital sex by women, and 65 percent disapproved of adult premarital sex by men. Fewer respondents disap-proved of sexual acts if the partners loved each other,—"leaving little doubt, therefore, that many respondents still cherished the ideal of love as a basis for sex-ual behavior, the authors said.[8]

According this survey, and reading from the last sentence, only a few number of respondents thought it was still wrong to have sexual acts even if the partners loved each other. Therefore, majority thought it was alright to have sex if love was the basis for that behavior. In a romantic relationship, who are the ones who suffer the most, when love turns out to be a fake one? In order to understand how love has changed in recent times, it is better to cast a quick glance at what love meant during past centuries. To be sure, history has never witnessed the sort of love that we are witnessing in our present era. True love has disappeared from the hearts of most people, and the meaning of this word, "love" has lost it's signifi-cance and glory. It seems to this writer that, true love may have been, to a large extent, displaced by fake love. It seems to him that it's this type of love that has found it's way into the hearts of some people. As a result, the word "love" has become adorned with beautiful colors of deception and tricks, just for the sake of achieving a particular objective. It seems this word is now being employed to plunder, kidnap or rape others. A lot of people may have already been victimized by love!

Certainly this has been the sorry state of love in this present era. There are some, who are silently eating the bitter fruit's of fake love; they are indeed, forced to swallow them; despite the fact that they are covered with "thorns". Fake love is always devoid of honesty and purity. So now where has true love 'emigrated' to?

---

8.   *China Post* (Taipei), 28 June 1989.

To the cemeteries perhaps! We all do hear news reports about social problems that have arisen due to illegal sexual relationships—sex has broken many homes than money ever did. Fake love has often engendered illegal sexual relationships that have often resulted in suicides, depression and even lunacy. In audiotapes broadcast in March 2004 in a two-part NBC News special, Diana, the Princess of Wales, described her early knowledge of Prince Charles' affair with Camilla Parker Bowles, her battle with bulimia, and several suicide attempts. "I threw myself down the stairs bearing in mind I was carrying a child," she said, describing one incident. "Queen (Elizabeth) comes out, absolutely horrified, shaking she's so frightened…and Charles went out riding."[9]

Diana continued, "I once heard him on the telephone in his bath…and he said, "Whatever happens, I'll always love you, and I told him I'd listened at the door…we had a filthy row." She later said her eating disorder "started the week after we got engaged." "My husband put his hand on my waistline and said: 'Oh, a bit chubby here, aren't we?' And that triggered off something in me," Diana said.[10] That had been the fate of a Princess who had touched the hearts of so many people around the world with love and compassion. From an Islamic viewpoint, a man who can't be content with only one wife is allowed to have a second wife—provided all the necessary conditions have been met. Some people still find it difficult to comprehend the concept of polygamy in Islam. Is it not sensible that instead of 'pretending' to love only one woman, a man honestly turns himself to be a true lover of two women? As unpleasant as it may be, reality dictates that there is not a woman in the planet who can fully satisfy the needs of a powerful male. When women quit asking men to make them the center of their universe and learn to accept a strong man's desire for more than one woman, families will live together longer, more happily and with little rancor.

It is sufficient to say here that polygamy existed in almost all nations and was even sanctioned by Judaism and Christianity until recent centuries. According to Dr. Jamal Badawi, the Qur'an is the only revealed scripture that explicitly limited polygamy and discouraged it's practice by various stringent conditions. He explains that, one of the reasons for not categorically forbidding polygamy is that in different places at different times, there may exist individual or social exigencies that make polygamy a batter solution than either divorce or a hypocritical monogamy while indulging in all types of illicit relations.[11] And even though

---

9.   *MSNBC, In tapes Diana speaks of marriage woes,* 1
10.   Ibid.
11.   Jamal Badawi, *The Status of Women in Islam,* (Plainfield: Department of Education and Training, MSA of U.S. and Canada, 1980), 19.

some Muslims may be corrupt, insincere and even fake lovers, the Qur'an seeks to train them to become true lovers in the following words:

> "If ye fear that ye shall not
> Be able to deal justly with the orphans,
> Marry women of your choice, two, or
> Three or four; but if ye fear that ye
> Shall not be able to deal (justly) with them,
> Then only one…that will be suitable…"[12]

Notice the conditional clause about orphans, introducing the rules about marriage. This reminds us about the immediate occasion of the promulgation of this verse. It was after the battle of Uhud—named after Mount Uhud, which dominates the city of Madinah (Saudi Arabia), some three miles to the north. It was a battle between the young Muslim community and the pagans of Mecca that took place in January 625 A. D. This battle left the Muslim community with many orphans and widows and some captives of war. Their treatment was to be governed by principles of greatest humanity and equity. The occasion is past but the principle remain—Marry the orphans if you are quite sure that you will in that way protect their interests and their property, with perfect justice to them and to your own dependents (if you have any). The unrestricted number of wives during the pre-Islamic period was now limited to a maximum of four—provided one could treat them with equality. My Chinese friends often say to me: "We know you Muslims can marry up to four wives is that true?" I always tell them that it's a way to train Muslims to be true and sincere lovers. And that it is the surest means to protect them from straying from the marital bed. However, I make them understand that "one man, one wife" is the golden rule; whereas "one man, four wives" is permissible but not recommended.

Having Sex is a Form of Worship

In Islam making love to one's lover (wife) is considered an act of worship and therefore rewarded by God. Many people including some Muslims misunderstand the concept of worship. Worship is commonly taken to mean performing ritualistic acts such as the five daily prayers, fasting in the month of Ramadan, giving charity to the poor and the needy, etc. This limited understanding is only

12.   Qur'an, 4: 3.

one part of the meaning of worship in Islam. The traditional definition of worship in Islam is a comprehensive definition that includes almost every thing in any individual's activities (including making love). Worship in Islam, therefore, is an all inclusive term for all that God loves of external and internal sayings and actions of a person. In other words, worship is everything one says or does for the pleasure of God. This of course includes rituals as well as beliefs, social activities and personal contributions to the welfare of one's fellow human beings. The Prophet of Islam, Muhammad (p.b.u.h.), said: "…and in the sexual act of each of you there is charity." They said: "O Messenger of God, when one of us fulfils his sexual desire, will he have some reward from that?" The Prophet said: "Do you [not] think that were he to act upon it unlawfully, he would be sinning?" Likewise if he has acted upon it lawfully he would have reward."[13] What this means is that sexual acts are rewarded if done lawfully and are sinful if done unlawfully. This is meant to protect both partners in a romantic relationship.

The Prophet indicated—albeit in few words, the relationship between love and sex by saying: "We have not seen anything better for lovers other than marriage."[14] This means that no love is true love if it falls short of marriage. In other words, at the top of the Love Mountain, one finds nothing but marriage. But how high is the Love Mountain? Or how far should one climb the Love Mountain before discovering marriage at the top? These questions will be answered in subsequent chapters. This saying of the Prophet is meant to protect both partners in a romantic relationship. The Prophet also indicated the relationship between love and sexual intercourse by advising his followers: "None of you should spring upon his lover (wife), in such a manner as the donkey does…" Rather, it's required of him to first of all engage her in amorous dalliance and laughter, so that the feelings of love and affection remains between the two. Thus in a romantic relationship, that inevitably leads to sexual intercourse, the Prophet advises his followers to pay particular attention to the other partner's feelings and yearnings through the medium of love. Therefore, a Muslim is not supposed to be a greedy lover, who is only interested in himself prior to, and after a sexual encounter with his wife. A sexual instinct that is satisfied in the manner described by the Prophet becomes encompassing if there exists a continuation of a cordial relationship between husband and wife, that sort of conjugal relationship that has been built upon the purity of purpose, mutual affection, and true love. Certainly, a complete union between two bodies and two souls becomes inseparable. You belong

---

13.   Related by *Muslim* in his authentic collections of the traditions of the Prophet.
14.   Related by *Ibn Majah* in his authentic collections of the traditions of the Prophet.

to her, and she belongs to you. In such a union, there is no room for one party to resort to double-dealing or trickery.

Sex is not a thing to be ashamed of, or to be treated lightly, or to be indulged in excess. Therefore, there is an advice for lovers dealing with sex in the Holy Book of the Muslims:

> "Your wives are
> As a tilth unto you
> So approach your tilth
> When or how ye will;
> But do some good act
> For your souls beforehand;
> And fear Allah,
> And know that ye are
> To meet Him (in the Hereafter),
> And give (these) good tidings
> To those who believe."[15]

The most delicate matters are here referred to in the most discreet and yet helpful terms. In sex, morality, manner, time and place are all important; and the highest standards are set by social laws, by our own refined instincts of mutual consideration (not by chicanery or peremptory commands); and above all, by the light shed by the Prophets from the wisdom which they receive from God, Who loves purity and cleanliness in all things. Sex is as solemn a fact as anything in life. It's compared to a husbandman's tilth; it's a serious affair to him: he sows the seeds in order to reap the harvest. But he chooses his own time and mode of cultivation. He does not sow out of season; the young man mentioned earlier had wanted to sow out of season by asking for a birthday present from a 13 year-old. Due to mutual love, a loving husband does not cultivate his tilth in such a manner as to injure or exhaust the soil (his wife). He is wise and considerate and does not run riot. Coming from the simile to human beings, every kind of mutual consideration is required, but above all, we must remember that even in those matters there is a spiritual aspect. We must never forget our souls, and that we are responsible to God.

---

15.   Qur'an, 2: 223.

It was carnal-minded men who invented the doctrine of original sin: "Behold" says the Psalmist. "I was shapen in iniquity, and in sin did my mother conceive me."[16] This is entirely repudiated by Islam, in which the office of father and mother is held in the highest veneration. Every child is born pure. In accordance with Islam, celibacy is not necessarily a virtue, (and may be a vice). Sometime ago, a Church of England report said: "living in sin" should no longer be regarded as sinful and the phrase should be dropped—given the number of people who now live together before marriage. "The phrase 'living in sin' stigmatizes and isn't helpful," said Bishop Alan Morgan, who chaired the first major study of the family by Britain's state religion for 20 years.[17] There are those who also think that sex isn't a crime. According to them, it's the motivation of the universe. They say that no psychologically or physically normal adult can resist it. But we have to remember that morals, after all, never change in time, what is right will always be right.

Islam does not base our knowledge of vice and virtue on mere intellect, desire, intuition or experience derived through the sense organs; which constantly undergo shifts, modifications and alterations; and do not provide definite, categorical and unchanging standards of morality. It provides us with a definite source—the Divine Revelation, as embodied in the Holy Qur'an, and the *Sunnah* (the way of life of the Prophet Muhammad, peace be upon him). These sources prescribe a standard or moral conduct that is permanent and universal and holds good in every age and under all circumstances. What prevents partners "living in sin" from tying the knot? Is it due to economic reasons or that one partner isn't sure if the other is really interested, or just that both have decided not to ever get married? How long do they plan to "live in sin"? Is it until death do they part? "Living in sin" negates the true meaning of love. Some people "living in sin" may have already considered the word "marriage" to be 'infectious' and must be avoided at all cost. They prefer to continue swimming (in the eyes of Islam), in the whirlpool of aberration. Reason is that, these days, it has become facile for men and women to satisfy their carnal desires without actually being in love. The consequences are what we see today.

---

16. *Psalm li.* 5.
17. *China Post* (Taipei), 11 June 1995.

Love and Sexual Infidelity

We are seeing with our eyes what AIDS is doing to mankind. Mankind has been fighting some diseases whose causes are known but whose cures are yet unknown. Two of such diseases are Leprosy and AIDS. Surely we have offended God so much so that should He decide to punish us, no one will be left on this planet. Note that in 13th century France, more than 2000 facilities were built to house sufferers of leprosy—a Biblical disease. However, the Biblical stigma remains so great that emotionally loaded terms like "leper" and "leprosy" are no longer used. It is now known as Hansen's disease, named after a Norwegian physician who first pinpointed the bacteria in 1873. It is possible that the "civilized" man may eventually destroy the world as we know it today. This destruction may result from diseases—not from Intercontinental Ballistic Missiles (ICBMs) or Nuclear Submarines. A disease like AIDS which alters the body metabolism and makes the patient become dry and slim must be dreaded and avoided. This has been the sorry state of the "civilized" man who has misplaced the true meaning of love. Our freewheeling "macho" attitudes toward sex would only push us toward extinction.

When the Holy Qur'an advises and teaches us the true meaning of love, it is not only dogmatizing, it is for our own safety. Our disobedience and arrogance will only bring us more trouble. In the Holy Qur'an, we read about the story of Prophet Yusuf (Joseph), in which we find how carnal love is contrasted with purity and chastity. The Qur'anic story is a highly spiritual sermon or allegory explaining the enduring nature of virtue in a world full of flux and change. Joseph was taken by a merchant into Egypt, was bought by a great Egyptian court dignitary (Aziz), who adopted him. The dignitary's wife sought, but in vain to attract Joseph to the delights of earthly love, which he resisted:

> "But she in which house
> He was, sought to seduce him
> She fastened the doors and said:
> 'Now come,'
> He said: 'God forbid!'
> Truly (thy husband) is my lord!
> He made my sojourn agreeable!'
> Truly to no good come those
> Who do wrong."[18]

The Egyptian court dignitary had treated Joseph with honor; he was more his guest and son than his slave. In trying to seduce Joseph in these circumstances, his wife closed the door in an attempt to hide her crime. Joseph was a stranger in the land of Egypt, had he "gone for it", no one would have known, and even if their act were to be discovered, he could have runaway from Egypt. More over, this was a slave being offered sex by his master's wife—an extremely beautiful woman. Needless to say, this was a moment when a slave was given an opportunity to share a woman with his master—an opportunity some of today's men, whether married or single would not squander. He was still innocent, and worst of all, he was threatened of imprisonment or severe punishment if he declined her "offer". Joseph had all the reasons to "go for it". Despite all these, he held fast to his faith in God and rose above his animal instinct. He was saved from this situation due to his knowledge of God and his faith in Him. The courtier's wife, on the other hand, was guilty of a crime against Joseph's honor and dignity. And there was a third fault in her earthly love. True love blots Self out. It thinks more of the loved one than of the Self. The courtier's wife was seeking the satisfaction of her own selfish passion. This was an instance whereby a married woman tried to cheat on her husband within the confines of her matrimonial home. Then do we say the courtier's wife did not love her husband when she married her in the first place? Something might have gone wrong somewhere.

The Qur'an describes the strong passion that blinded this woman who only wanted to satisfy her sexual instinct without thinking of it's consequences:

> "And (with passion) did she
> Desire him, and he would
> Have desired her, but that
> He saw the evidence of
> His Lord: thus (did We order)
> That we might turn away from
> Him (all) evil and indecent deeds
> For he was one of our servants chosen."[19]

She was blinded with passion, and his plea had no effect on her. Joseph was human after all and her passionate love and her beauty placed a great temptation in his path. But he had a sure refuge—his faith in God. His spiritual eyes saw

---

18.   Qur'an,12: 23.
19.   Qur'an, 12: 24.

something that her eyes, blinded by passion, did not see. She thought no one saw when the door was closed. But Joseph knew that God was there. That made him strong and proof against temptation. The credit of our being saved from sin is due, not to our weak earthly nature, but to God. We can only try, like Joseph, to be true and sincere; God will purify and save us from all that is wrong. Tempted, yes. But we rise above ourselves. If you love someone, you naturally obey him or her. Yes Joseph was tempted, but his love for God, which according to Islam must be above all love prevented him from succumbing to the wiles of this woman who had something of the dog in her—she radiated ethereal beauty as if though not of this world!

During my sojourn in one African country, one of my friends there told me how he sometimes hear some women complain about their love lives. "These days, if you don't have a 'spare driver' your husband wouldn't respect you." They are sometimes heard saying. Being a bit inquisitive, I asked my friend what the expression, "spare driver" meant. To my utter dismay he said it meant having another lover. Add to this the following expression; "one man's wife could be another man's lover." As we all know, a spare driver isn't the main driver. He is the assistant driver. His services will only be needed if the main driver is indisposed. In their case, their husbands were to be considered the "main drivers". The worst thing was that these "drivers" were not aware they had "spare drivers". No man would like to share his wife with a "spare driver", unless of course he isn't aware of him. This is just an example of how far some married people have gone away from the true meaning of love. Does a woman truly love her husband if she hires a "spare driver"? How is she going to 'pay' him?

My question to this "spare driver" is, Is your love for a married woman built upon sincerity, purity and affection, or that it's only built upon satisfying your sexual instincts through an illegal way? What would be your fate if you get caught by your "boss"? To the married woman seriously searching to recruit a "spare driver", If your love for your husband is going to be shared by a "spare driver" then why would you get married to that man in the first place? Then why do you hope to raise a responsible family in such a matrimonial home that is shared between your husband and your "spare driver"? Oh no! From the Islamic viewpoint, you are rattling the wrong cage of love! Your love for your husband is not characteristic of true love that is based upon affection, compassion, tenderness and humility. Because it's only out of a dignified and true love that a matrimonial home must be built upon. Because with a dignified and true love comes the fusion of the hearts and souls of both of you. Thereafter, you begin to act like one individual. Then of course, the rainbow of love engulfs you—cultivating in you, the acceptance, with proud equanimity the misfortunes of life. You and your husband are meant to be together through thick and thin.

In Islam, married couples are expected to be best friends who enjoy being with each other more than with anyone else. They have the same goals, devote time to sharing their most intimate thoughts, and if one has a passionate pastime, the other learns to like it. This doesn't mean that husband and wife can't possess different personality trait's (like watching night baseball vs. making love all night), Rather couples should strive to know each other very well so that, they internalize the other's thoughts and values. If you don't think a bit like your partner, you will never understand each other. Love, after all is compassion and humility. In the case of this woman thinking of 'hiring' a "spare driver", if you had internalized and accepted your husband, there would have been very little that could tear both of you apart. It could be that your husband is a philanderer and you want to retaliate. It could also be that, your spouse is incapable of "heating up" the marital bed. But because of the fundamental unshakable bond you vowed to uphold together before marriage, you should have sat down with your husband to discuss how best both of you could light up your love life.

This writer has a firm belief that everyone, no matter his or her circumstances, has the natural right to enjoy the world's beauty and joie de vivre. In the Holy Qur'an we are reminded of this joie de vivre:

> "And among His signs is this,
> That He has created for you
> Mates from among yourselves,
> That ye may dwell in tranquility
> With them, and He has put love
> And mercy between your (hearts)
> Verily in that are signs for those
> Who reflect."[20]

This Qur'anic verse refers to the wonderful mystery of sex. Children arise out of the union of the sexes. And it's always the female that brings forth the offspring—whether female or male. And the father is as necessary as mother for bringing forth daughters. Unregenerate man is pugnacious in the male sex, but rest and tranquility are found in the normal relations of both parents living

---

20. Qur'an, 30:21.

together and raising a family. A man's gallantry to the opposite sex is natural and God-given. The friendship of two men between each other is quite different in quality and temper from the feeling which unspoiled nature expects as between men and women. There is a special kind of love and tenderness between them. And as a woman is the weaker sex, that tenderness may, from a certain aspect, be likened to mercy, the protecting kindness that the strong should give to the weak. The husband is expected to cater to the sexual needs of his wife and vice-versa. You suck each other dry. In a loving relationship, Islam expects couples to grow together—not grow apart. A man with a hyperactive libido can always find solace in a loving wife.

In the Holy Qur'an, God calls mankind to remember their duties to Him and to conduct their love affairs in a just and respectful manner:

> "O mankind! be conscious
> Of your guardian Lord,
> Who created you from
> A single person, created
> Out of it, his mate, and
> From them twain scattered
> (Like seeds), countless men
> And women…and be heedful
> Of the wombs (that bore you)…"[21]

The mystery of sex is here again stated by God in the Holy Qur'an. The impenitent male is apt, in the pride of his physical strength, to forget the all-important role that the female plays in his very existence and in all our social relationships that arise in our collective human lives. The mother that bore us must ever have our reverence. The wife, through whom we enter parentage, must have our reverence. Sex, which governs so much of our physical life, and has so much influence on our emotional and higher nature, deserves not our fear, or our contempt, or our amused indulgence, but our reverence in the highest sense of the term. The fact that some Muslim men treat their wives as slave girls is a shame. On the other hand, some media propaganda against the ill treatment of Muslim women is ludicrous. Indeed it's born out of ignorance regarding the status of women in Islam.

---

21.   Qur'an, 4:1.

This "spare driver" scenario is comparable to the story of *Majnoun,* a lunatic (in Arabic), and his lover called Layla narrated in *Kitaabul-Aghani* (The Book of Songs), by Al- Asfahani.[22] In it, the narrator, Khalid ibn Hamal tells us of how this lunatic was madly in love with a woman called Layla. This lunatic had met Layla on several occasion before, and even after her marriage to another man. We are told in this book that when Layla's husband and her father traveled out of town, she sent her slave girl to fetch her lover—that lunatic. He spent the night with her, but was sent away before sunrise. Before she had her "lover" sent away she said to him: "Come to me every night, as long as the travelers have not returned." As widely expected, this lunatic continued seeing her nightly, until the travelers returned.

It could be said that *Majnoun* did what he did because he couldn't get married to Layla. But after her marriage to another man, it would have been proper for him to end that relationship and transfer his loving to another woman other than Layla. *Majnoun's* infatuation for Layla was so intense that he gave up the five daily prayers that Muslims are obligated to do. His love for Layla had replaced his fear of God. This is what the narrator tells us in this book "…He did not put on any garment; unless he had already torn it into pieces; he did not walk (in the streets) unless he was stark naked; he played with earth, and gathered bones around himself and, if you mentioned Layla to him, he would become boisterous; and would begin to narrate to you every detail about her. But if you asked him: "Why did you give up the five daily prayers? He would not utter a single word…"[23] But is this the way a love affair should be conducted? If it were to be that way then customs and values would be lost between people. And all that is known as congeniality, affection, compassion and tenderness would have been lost. Consequently, a lover would have lost that deep-rooted tranquility; he or she aspires for, in a romantic relationship.

Why did Layla, despite her love for *Majnoun* (the lunatic), failed to marry him? Was she afraid she would be scoffed at, for getting married to a lunatic? It's strange that she would allow him sneak into her matrimonial home during the darkness of the night. She preferred only to have sex with him but not marry him. The question is, What was so special about *Majnoun* that drove Layla crazy? Was Layla's lawful husband incapable of satisfying her sexual needs? How could a lunatic manage to "heat up" Layla's marital bed in a way better than her husband

---

22. Abdul Halim Muhammad Qanbas, *Al Hubb Fil-Islam* (Damascus: Dar Al-Hikmah, 1977), 38 quoting Al-Isfahani, *Kitabul Aghani* (n. d.).
23. Ibid., 40.

did? The probable answer could have been that, Layla loved *Majnoun* for sex, but kept her husband for security and dignity. There may be such other "Laylas" in every nook and cranny of this earth. These are married women who would not seek divorce from their husbands, but at the same time would like to hold fast to their *Majnouns*. The general idea is clear—husbands for security, *Majnouns* for sex! Then again we are confronted with a dilemma: Is love really blind as some often say? If it were the case, Why didn't Layla marry *Majnoun* and forget of the world around her? Where should we draw the line between love and sex? All along this writer has said that true love should culminate in marriage. But this is the case where by those supposed to be true lovers are themselves involved in cheating. It could be that either of the married partners is cheating on the other, or both cheating on one another.

In his essay on *The Behavior Of Married Couples,* Charles Lamb (1775-1834), a prominent English literary critic wrote: "Nothing is to me more distasteful than that entire complacency and satisfaction which beam in the countenances of a newly-married couple." This complacency and satisfaction shown by newly-weds could soon change into diffidence and frustration if the foundation of this marriage is deficient in true love. There are sufficient reasons for every one involved in a romantic relationship to remain circumspect and avoid complacency. The challenge always is, How do we create the good times for true lovers, and get these good times rolling? It all boils down to three basic facts: who gets *what, when* and *how* in a romantic relationship? The *what, when* and *how* questions, if considered carefully by true lovers would definitely create the good times for them, not only that, it would keep these good times rolling for years on end. In a romantic relationship, *who* gets the sex, the care, the respect, the warmness, and consideration? *How* does she or he want to get them? *When* does she or he want to have them? In a romantic relationship, both partners do have special needs at specific times and in a particular manner. In a romantic relationship, partners are expected to be tactful, to know how to act in any given situation. In a nutshell, savoir-faire is an exceedingly important asset of a man or woman in love. Sometimes, even the most successful marriage could be wrecked due to a lack of savoir-faire.

In an attempt to create good times for lovers, and keep these good times rolling, the Almighty God instructs us through His Prophet Muhammad in the Holy Qur'an as follows:

> "The adulterer cannot have
> Sexual relations with any but

An adulteress, or an idolatress,
And the adulteress, none can
Have sexual relations with her
But an adulterer or an idolater;
To the believers such a thing
Is forbidden."[24]

Islam commands sex purity, for men and for women, at all times—before marriage, during marriage, and after the dissolution of marriage. Those guilty of illicit practices are to be encouraged to give them up, so that they become accepted into the marriage circle of chaste men and women. And with this, there is a clear and an unambiguous line drawn between love and sex. In a telephone survey conducted by EDKA Associates, and carried by the *Rocky Mountain News*–USA, two out of three women would want to be virgins if they were getting married today, and half believe neither men nor women should have any sexual experience before wedlock. Researchers also found that 53 percent of the 500 women questioned said they believe that having sex for the first time with your future spouse, is just as chaste as waiting for your wedding day; 42 percent disagreed.[25]

We discern from the foregoing that falling in love with someone you think you love doesn't automatically mean having a carte blanche to indulge in sexual escapades with him or her. As far as LOVE and SEX are concerned, some of the regrets we often have to deal with in our love lives come from saying "yes" too soon [to love] and "no" too late [to sex].

24. Qur'an, 24:3.
25. *Rocky Mountain News,* "Would You Rather Be A Virgin? Most Women Say Yes," *Woman's Own,* December 1994, 21.

2

THE MEANING OF LOVE

No matter who we fall in love with, we all face the dilemmas of love. To be sure, most of us question love throughout life. "Does my husband really love me? Won't he abandon me in the cause of time for a much younger wife? These days he always returns home late from work..., and when I attempt to ask him why, he yells at me, is he having an affair?" One housewife lamented. "Is my boy friend serious about marriage? Why is it that when ever I bring up the subject of marriage he tries to change the topic, yet; every morning, he tells me he feels like a robin that has just caught the first worm of spring, and that he loves me more than the previous day...yet; he only takes interest in 'sliding between the sheets with me', he is hesitant to slip a ring on my finger, he says he loves me, more and not less; what sort of love is this?" Another woman complained bitterly.

In her letter to an advice corner, one reader wrote: "My boyfriend and I have been a couple for five months and are very much in love. He is wonderful and attractive, and the sweetest man I've ever dated. He takes care of my car problems, flat tires, anything I need, and I help him in his business, make him dinner, anything he needs, we see each other everyday. He is the man of my dreams. My problem is that I'm ready to talk marriage, and he doesn't seem to be. He is 10 years older than me and has been married twice before, both times to women who turned out NOT to be nice people and about whom he had misgivings even before tying the knot. I've never been married before, and I do take it very seriously. My bringing up the subject has been a killer of other relationships in the past, and this one, I don't want to kill. Subsequently, I'm afraid to bring it up. We share the same religion and believe that premarital sex is wrong...I vacillate between two camps: thinking I need to back off and prepare to date other people, or the idea that, OK, being his girl friend is definitely better than any other man's wife..."[1]

---

1.   *China Post* (Taipei), 9 April 2004.

Some General Assumptions

We often hear phrases like: "Love is like a chicken soup, because chicken soup is heartwarming and nourishing just like love; love can't be defined, it can only be felt; love is like a morning smile; love is when there is no time; love is like the long wait for eternity; love is like a woman in one touch, etc." It's also essential to examine some of the famous sayings about love. *Love is Blind.* This proverb first came into existence through the poetry narrated by Geoffrey Chaucer (1340?–1400).[2] He was considered the most famous English playwright before the advent of William Shakespeare (1564–1616). Chaucer wrote *The Canterbury Tales.* After Chaucer came Shakespeare who said in one of his plays—*Two Gentlemen of Verona* (1592).

> "If you love her you cannot see her
> Why? Because love is blind."[3]

What is meant here usually refers to the inability of a lover to discern the shortcomings in the one he or she loves. In other words, lovers faintly discern each other's shortcomings. Later on Shakespeare re-adjusted this meaning in another play: *The Merchant of Venice* (1596).

> "But love is blind, and lovers cannot see
> The pretty follies that themselves commit."[4]

Therefore, when we say love is blind, it means lovers are unwilling or unable to understand or notice the shortcomings in each other. In other words, love that is blind is love without reason or judgement—it just happens for no any other reason. Indeed, it's love that's not ruled by purpose; it's thoughtless and reckless. Let's pause for a moment and ask ourselves, Is love really blind in the real world? Credit Robert Schuman, a French Statesmen (1886–1963), said: "When I was young, I vowed never to get married until I find an ideal woman, well, I found her, but unfortunately, she had been waiting for a perfect man." Undoubtedly, The heart of this honorable Statesman was at an "auction" waiting for the highest "bidder". After waiting for so long, he finally did find a woman whom he

---

2.   Munir Ba'albaki, *Al-Mawrid: A Modern English-Arabic Dictionary*, 32nd ed., (Beirut: Dar El-ilm Lil-Malayen, 1998), Section on Proverbs (in Arabic), 62.

3.   Ibid.

4.   Ibid., 62.

[wrongly] thought could be the highest "bidder". To his amazement, this ideal woman didn't even realize his presence at that "auction". Not even the "auction-eer" could draw the attention of this ideal "bidder" to the Frenchman. What a pity! Why is it that there is now a growing number of single women who would rather prefer to stay single and happy, than give their hearts to undeserved men who would only cause them more pain and suffering? This writer thinks only a few people nowadays still believe in the notion of love being blind.

Ernest Hemingway (1899-1961), the American writer and Nobel Laureate in Literature (1954) said: "Never worry about women; just try and be kind and good and think in their head and make them happy. If they are bitches you can always dump them. Most women aren't bitches except when they are made so by men." The other famous saying goes as: "Love me, love my dog." The meaning of this is that if someone loves a person, he or she should also love all things dearest to him or her. And that a person in love should protect the possessions of his or her sweetheart, as well as look after the welfare of him or her. A Christian Priest, St. Bernard, reportedly said in the year 1153:"*Que me amat, amat et canem meum.*" This means that, "Anyone who loves me also loves my dog." And in the year 1480, another famous saying about love went as follows: "*He that lovythe me lovythe my hound.*"[5] A hound is a type of dog used for hunting; foxhound. There is a common saying in French West Africa about love: *Pas la jalousie, pas l'amour.* "If there is no jealousy, then there is no love." Love and jealousy are strange bed-fellows and if a man loves a woman he will always be restless if he sees her talking to a stranger, and vice versa.

In pre-Islamic Arabia—the period before the advent of Islam—which some Western writers consider to be "the Age of Ignorance or Barbarism," and which they thought to be between the years (500–622 A.C. 'After Christ')[6], the woman's position was indeed unenviable; though she participated in many a social and economic activity, and though, sometimes, glowing tributes were paid to sweethearts in pre-Islamic poetry; generally, women were treated as chattels. There was no limit to a man taking as many wives as he liked. Similarly, he divorced his wives at will and quite frequently. There was no rule of prohibition; so a man could, and did marry irrespective of blood relationship. Often two sis-ters were joined as wives to a man at the same time. Sons married their fathers' ex-wives or widows (not mothers). The Birth of a daughter was considered inaus-

---

5.   Ibid.,63
6.   Muhammad Mohar Ali, *Siral Al-Nabi And the Orientalists*, vol. 1A(Madina: King Fahd Complex for the Printing of the Holy Qur'an and Center for the Service of the Sunna, 1997), 64.

picious and disliked.[7] Most inhumane was that many Arabs, out of false sense of honor and for fear of poverty, buried alive their young daughters.[8] Despite the ill treatment of women, this was what a pre-Islamic poet called, Al-Munakhal al–Yashkuri had to say about love:

> "And I love her and she loves me
> "And her she camel loves my camel."[9]

What al-Yashkuri wanted to convey to us was that the love between he and his sweetheart was so intense and pervasive that it caused their two camels (male and female) to also fall in love with each other. This was in spite of the fact that he (and other men like him) during that epoch could marry and divorce their sweethearts at will without the slightest compunction.

A man in love might say to his sweetheart: "I love you more than the love ants have for one another." This may be an hyperbole, indeed, it might just be a meretricious expression, with no real feeling behind it. It's only recently that researchers have found out that the "fire of love" between ants is several times hotter than that between human beings. It has been found out by Scientists that every act of interaction between ants springs from their lofty and very sincere love for each other. In effect, ants have a love for each other that can't be found in any other creature on earth.

The Islamic Concept

The Qur'an, the Holy book of the Muslims which contains the word of God that was revealed to the unlettered Prophet Muhammad (peace be upon him) hinted about fourteen hundred years ago the love between ants. The twenty-seventh chapter of the Holy Qur'an is called *An-Naml* in Arabic, or "The Ants" in English. In this chapter, and in verse 18, we read the following:

> "At length, when they came
> To a valley of ants,

---

7.   Qur'an, 16: 58-59.
8.   Qur'an, 6:137: 6:151.
9.   Ba'albaki, *Al-Mawrid*, 63.

One of the ants said:

'O ye ants, get into
Your habitations, lest Solomon
And his hosts crush you
(Under foot) without knowing it.'"[10]

The ant, to outward appearance is a very small and humble creature. In the great pomp and circumstances of the world of lovers, she (generic feminine in Arabic) may be neglected or even trampled on by lovers who mean her no harm, yet by her sincere love and wisdom, she carries on her own life full of love within her own sphere ("Habitations"), with unalloyed enthusiasm.

The biological and physical facts of the universe could not have been known before modern technological break-through. How could Muhammad (peace be upon him), an unlettered prophet, describe what goes on between ants? It's unfortunate that many people are unaware of the intense love between ants and, as a result, treat their wives as if they were chattels. The rising divorce rate in some Muslim communities around the world is unacceptable, and stands as a betrayal of the teachings of the Holy Qur'an. A Christian friend of mine, out of sheer ignorance and prejudice looked up to me and said: "I know you Muslims don't respect your wives." Although, this remark was unfair and acrimonious, I accepted his verdict with grace and style; knowing very well that these criticisms are true to a certain extent.

Love is a word that is being uttered by every human being, sometimes without knowing it's true significance. True love trembles the heart, it makes the tongue incapable of expressing the true nature of the feelings that are deep-rooted in the innermost recesses of the heart. Love is a word that obtained the status of "sweetness" since the beginning of mankind. It is an expression of the feeling of tenderness and affection. It has no any abode other than inside the heart. True love makes the limbs speak either verbally or physically. Allah (the proper name of God in Arabic), kept love in the hearts of mankind since He created them, in order that, it (love) helps them in facing the vicissitudes of life on earth, and also help them face every difficulty.

Love could be categorized into two basic degrees of intensity: True love, which is the most intense and springs forth from the innermost core of the heart. And fake love, that is of a lower intensity. It may be ostentatious and may not have a place inside the heart. It's the worst form of love. There is no doubt that for every

---

10.   Qur'an, 27:18.

coin, there are two faces; and in romance, there is true love and fake love. In The Holy Qur'an, we read this verse:

> "Glory to God, Who created
> In pairs all things that
> The earth produces, as well as
> Their own (human) kind
> And (other) things of which
> They have no knowledge."[11]

There are positive and negative forces in the universe; good and evil; life and death; black and white; happiness and sorrow; male and female. I think Sir Isaac Newton (1643–1729), the famous English Physicist confirmed this in his law in physics, when he wrote: "For every action, there is an equal and opposite reaction." The same applies to love; true and fake love. It's not everybody who says "I love you" is really a true lover, at least, from the Islamic perspective. The Prophet of Islam, Muhammad (peace be upon him) made a famous description about true love when he said:

> "We have not seen anything better
> for lovers other than marriage."[12]

This means that every romantic relationship should end in marriage. In other words, marriage is what is to be found at the top of the Love Mountain. Therefore, according to Islam, love is imperfect if either (or both) of the lovers aren't interested in tying the knot. We know Diana, The People's Princess was a true lover when she wrote: "I never wanted a divorce and always dreamed of a happy marriage with loving support from Charles…a part of me will always love Charles." This was at a time she was going through a painful divorce with Charles, the Prince of Wales. Charles, the heir to the throne, married 20 year-old Lady Diana Spencer at a pomp—laden service in St. Paul's Cathedral in 1981. But the marriage foundered in part over Diana's unhappiness with Charles continuing relationship with his companion Camilla Parker Bowles.

---

11.   Qur'an, 36: 36.
12.   Narrated by *Ibn Majah*, one of the leading authorities in *Hadith* (The Prohet's traditions).

Love is like a bat, and by analogy, it's eyes compare favorably with fake love whereas it's wings compare favorably with true love. Naturally, the bat keeps hidden in the daylight, although, daylight reveals everything else, and gets moving in the night, although night shuts up every other living being. The bat keeps it's eyelids down in the day, and instead treat night as a lamp. The darkness of the night does not obstruct the sight of the bat nor does the gloom of darkness prevent it from movement. However, as soon as the sun removes it's veil and the light of morning appears, and the rays of it's light enter upon the lizards in their holes, the bat pulls down its eyelids. This has been the case because, the bat's eyes gets dazzled during the daytime. It cannot make use of the light of the sun for being guided in it's movements and for reaching it's known abode. In effect, the brightness of daylight is of no use to the bat's eyes. Fake love is devoid of spiritual guidance. The Qur'an says: *Yakaadul-barqu Yakhtafu Absaarahum* (The lightning all but snatches away their sight).[13]

On the other hand, true love is like the wings of the same bat. These wings are made of flesh, they look like the ends of ears without feathers or bones. You can see the veins quite distinctly. These wings are neither too thin to get turned over during flying, nor too thick to prove heavy. When the bat flies, the young ones hold on to these wings, seeking refuge with them. The young does not leave these wings until it's own limbs and wings get strong that can bear it for rising up and flying too, and when it begins to recognize it's places of living and it's interests. True love is analogous to what the Qur'an terms as *Janaaha-zhulli mina rrahma* (a wing of tenderness and humility).[14]

The Holy Qur'an says about two (married) lovers:

> "…They are your garments
> And ye are their garments…"[15]

This is an eloquent description of true love. The fabric used in making this garment is love; the threads used in sewing it is love; and finally, the embroidery on the garment is love. Men and women are each other's garment. They are for mutual support; mutual comfort; mutual protection; fitting into each other as a garment fit's the body. Let's bear in mind that the "garments" mentioned above are custom-made. They are supposed to be made as the buyer specifies. In other words, you would not buy a garment you don't love. You would not become a

---

13.   Qur'an, 2:20.
14.   Qur'an, 17:24.
15.   Qur'an, 2:187.

garment for someone you don't love. This is a clear indictment against those Muslims who force their young girls to marry men they would otherwise not marry. There should never be a marriage that is devoid of mutual love. Much to my indignation, this practice is still very common in some Muslim communities in Africa (and even in some parts of the Middle East).

A person completely infatuated with someone else could still be considered to be a fake lover, because he or she has only been attracted to the opposite sex and it could be that the one being admired isn't even aware of it. It could also happen that there be a mutual attraction. This mutual attraction could cause in them a slight and burning sensation and a desire to get together. But it soon ends after either of them leaves the scene. For love to be said to be a true one, it must be felt in the hearts of both parties. True love is all-inclusive and pervasive than mere infatuation. If you truly love someone, you love everything about him or her. Do not say: "I admire him or her", because your admiration of someone could be dependent upon a particular characteristic or trait in the one being admired. For instance: "I admire her for her eloquence; I admire his round face or big eyes". Your admiration for this person could make tears drop down freely from your cheeks, and make the rest of your day dreamy and relaxed; yet still, you will not be said to have fallen headlong in love. No matter the intensity of your admiration it does not reach the degree of true love.

As a secondary school student in Ghana, some of our co-eds, in their admiration for some us, used to say to us: "Only your height; only your eyes; or only your nose." However, if some of us asked them out, they would politely decline. We used to be captivated by their generous compliments, and for one reason or another, wrongly thought they were actually in love with some of us. The reality was that, they were only attracted to some particular characteristics inherent in some of us and nothing more. Therefore, there exists a great difference between someone who is (temporarily) filled with intense love for you, and the one who truly loves you. True love, which has been advocated by Islam, is more pristine and more deep-rooted than admiration. When asked, which was more commendable, infatuation or love? the Islamic scholar, Abul Abbas Ahmad, the son of Yahya said: "Love is more commendable, because infatuation could be pretentious that might finally lead to flippancy; as for love, it does not disappear from the heart of the lover, but stays there and increases in intensity, even if a meeting between the two has ended."[16]

---

16.   Qanbas, *Al Hubb Fil-Islam,* 29.

Therefore, from the above clarification, and from an Islamic point of view, being infatuated with someone cannot be equated to being in love. You are only an admirer and would not necessarily qualify as a true lover. It may be that either of the two is involved in a hanky-panky relationship. Either of the two lovers is often guilty of exaggerating his or her love for the other. This type of relationship cannot battle the vicissitudes of life. On the other hand, true love endures forever. The marked difference between a fake lover and a true lover is the longevity and intensity of his or her relationship with the opposite sex. Relationships between "lovers" could be intense but short—indeed as short as a one night stand. It could also last longer, but would still lack the closeness or intensity associated with true lovers.

The luster of gold must not inveigle any true relationship down the road of betrayal. It's well important to have a spiritual peace as well as a material well being; it would, therefore, be nice if lovers could maintain their relationships with morality and conscience.

3

THE SOURCE OF EVERY LOVE

In accordance with Muslim belief, the source of all love is the only one true God Who exists necessarily, by Himself, encompassing all the excellent Divine Attributes of perfection. God is One and Unique, He has no partner, no equal. He does not beget, nor was he begotten. He does not inhere in anything, nothing inheres in Him. He is the sole Creator and Sustainer of all that exists. He is the One God, besides whom there is no other god. And there is none worthy of worship save Him. He has no wife, no son, and no father. He has no form or no material substance. He does not sleep nor does he take rest. He is the First with no beginning, and the Last with no end. He is the All-knowing who knows all that passes the hearts of lovers. He is the Omnipotent who has the free will that is not restrained by any power. When He desires a thing to be, He says, "Be" and it is. He is also the Beneficent, the Kind, and the Merciful, Whose love for mankind is seventy times greater than that of a mother for her child.

The God of Islam

The God of Islam is neither remote nor abstract. He is the Real Lord of the universe, whose love swells the heart and intoxicates the soul. Those who seek Him do not have to depend on the vicarious conviction of a priest, or the arguments in the books, to assure them that He exists. They can feel His existence in themselves, as well as in both animate and inanimate objects around them. And this is not the prerogative of the "spiritualists". Any layman who follows His guidance and seeks His presence will find Him close to himself. It's for this reason that, people of all sorts—intellectuals, scientists, priests, as well as people from all walks of life enter into the fold of Islam everyday. In Islam lovers find a God who responds to their call. But how did the Muslims get to know God, the Source of

31

all love? It was through the chain of prophets, starting with Adam, who was the first True Lover to his wife—Eve, and ended with Muhammad. Some prominent Prophets were Nuh (Noah), Ibrahim (Abraham), Musa (Moses), and Isa (Jesus). God's peace and blessing be upon them all. These prophets were humans; they ate, slept and had wives (except Jesus, who will marry at his second coming). These prophets were all true lovers.

This writer's claim that Muhammad (p.b.u.h.), for example, was a true lover can be deduced from the fact that, he remained faithful to his wife Khadija—who was fifteen years older than him—until her death. James A. Michener writes about him "...At twenty he was already a successful businessman, and soon became director of camel caravans for a wealthy widow. When he reached twenty-five his employer, recognizing his merit, proposed marriage. Even though she was fifteen years older, he married her, and as long as she lived remained a devoted husband..."[1] Muhammad (p.b.u.h) was the final Prophet sent by God. Born in Mecca 570 years after his predecessor Jesus (peace be upon him), he was up until the age of forty indistinguishable from any other man except that his extreme honesty had earned him the appellation "the Trustworthy". *The Encyclopedia Britannica* says about him: "a mass of detail in the early sources shows that he was an honest and upright man who had gained the respect and loyalty of others who were like-wise honest and upright men."[2]

Another writer, Michael H. Hart, had this to say about him: "My choice of Muhammad to lead the list of the world's most influential persons may surprise some readers and may be questioned by others, but he was the only man in history who was supremely successful on both the religious and secular level."[3] He was unlettered. And, although every religion of the world was named after it's founder, or after the community or nation in which it was born, this was not the case with the prophet of Islam. For instance, Christianity takes it's name from it's prophet Jesus Christ (p.b.u.h); Buddhism from it's founder, Gautama Buddha; Zoroastrianism from it's founder, Zoroaster; and Judaism, the religion of the Jews, from the name of the tribe Judah (of the country of Judea) where it originated. "Muhamedanism" is indeed a misnomer. Islam is the name of the religion. Islam, in fact is an attributive title. Anyone who possesses this attribute, whatever

1.   James A. Michener, "Islam: The Misunderstood Religion," *Reader's Digest* May 1955, 68-70.
2.   *The Encyclopedia Britannica* 11th ed., 609.
3.   Michael H. Hart, *The 100: A Ranking of the Most Influential Persons in History,*(New York: Hart Publishing Company, 1978), 33.

race, community, country, or group he or she belongs to, is a Muslim. Islam is an Arabic word and connotes submission, surrender and obedience to God.

Muhammad and the Qur'an

Having briefly discussed about God, Muhammad, and Islam, it's important that we mention the Holy Qur'an, that was revealed to Muhammad. One might be tempted to ask: "How authentic is this Book (the Qur'an), that makes Muslims hold it in so high an esteem, Is it not just an autobiography of Muhammad"? The Qur'an is divine in origin. It was revealed to the Prophet in short and long passages over a period of 23 years by the Archangel Jibreel (Gabriel). As it was revealed the Prophet committed each and every passage to memory. The Qur'an it's self bears testimony to the fact that early in his career he sometimes became so eager to commit the revealed text to memory that he hurriedly repeated the words as the Angel uttered them. He was divinely asked not to do so. And was assured that God would enable him to retain in his memory whatever was revealed to him. Many of his companions also memorized the revealed sacred texts. They had the immediate need to do so because they had to recite the passages in the five daily prayers that was made incumbent upon them from the very beginning of Islam. In the course of time, the Prophet as well as many of his ardent followers had the entire Qur'an committed to memory.

In Arabia in those days, as well as many other places in the world, there were no memory chips; so it was a widespread practice to memorize whole texts and literary works, genealogies and traditions, and to transmit them orally to subsequent generations. The desert Arabs were specially gifted with the skill of memorization. At intervals, particularly in the Holy Month of Ramadan (fasting), the prophet recited the whole Qur'an, as far as it was revealed, to the Archangel Gabriel; and it was on record that during the last Ramadan of his life he recited the entire Qur'an twice before that Angel. It was also during his lifetime that he arranged the passages of the Qur'an into it's present form—in accordance with divine guidance received through Gabriel. Not that the Qur'an was committed only to memory. The Prophet took early care to have the passages of the Qur'an written on suitable and available materials like tree leaves, bark, hides, bones, stones and such other objects.

In deed the impetus to have the texts written down was given in the very first revelation to the Prophet which emphasized, among other things, the acquisition and preservation of knowledge by means of the pen. The first direct revelation was:

"Proclaim! (Read!)
In the name
Of thy Lord and Cherisher,
Who created…He Who taught
The use of the pen.
Taught man that
He knew not."[4]

The declaration or proclamation was to be in the name of God the Creator. It was not for any personal benefit of the Prophet; to him, there was to come bitter persecution, sorrow and suffering. It was the call of God for the benefit of erring humanity. God is mentioned by His title of "thy Lord and Cherisher." From this first direct revelation to the Prophet, God, as the source of all love, mercy and tenderness, is made patently obvious—"the Cherisher". If you cherish someone in a romantic relationship, you protect or tend him or her lovingly; you care for him or her; you are fond of him or her; you keep the feelings of being together (and never separating) in your mind with pleasure. The message was not merely an abstract proposition of philosophy, but the direct concrete message of God to the creatures who He loves and cherishes.

God teaches us new knowledge at every given moment. Individuals learn more and more day by day; nations and humanity at large learn fresh knowledge at every stage. All our knowledge and capacities come as gifts from "the Cherisher". But man, in his inordinate vanity and insolence, mistakes "the Cherisher's" gifts for his own achievements. The gift may be strength or beauty, wealth, position, military and economic power, or the more subtle gifts of knowledge or talents in individuals; or Science or Art, or Government, or Organization for mankind in general. Man is not self-sufficient, either as an individual, or in his collective capacity.

The main justification for the revelation of the Qur'an was that, the earlier revealed books had been corrupted and altered by their followers, it was only natural that the Prophet should have been doubly careful to take appropriate steps to guard against such an eventuality in the case of the Qur'an. Indeed, the Qur'an it's self points to this fact and declares it's absolute integrity and immunity from external interference and interpolation

---

4.   Qur'an, 96: 1-5.

"It is a Book of stupendous authority
No falsehood can approach it
From before or behind it:
It is sent down by One
Full of Wisdom, Worthy of all Praise."[5]

Thus the Qur'an was preserved in memory as well as in writing. The process of writing down the text started early enough, almost simultaneously with the beginning of the revelation. The Prophet employed a number of his followers as copyists of the Qur'anic Texts. Written records of the revealed texts were kept with the Prophet as well as with many of his followers. A remarkable distinction of the Qur'an as a historical record is that unlike other records of a contemporary or near-contemporary nature, and unlike autobiographies, it was not "classified" and made privy to only some selected individuals for reasons of "national security". On the contrary, it was meant for immediate "declassification", publication and communication to the masses, and was in fact so published and communicated. This fact is important for two main reasons. First it militates against the suggestion made by the critics of Islam and of the Prophet that he "revised", modified or "altered" the text of the Qur'an with the progress of his mission as he advanced in knowledge and experience. For, if he did modify or alter the texts from time to time as "national constitutions are being amended", from time to time, even his followers, not to speak of his opponents would have found fault with him and would almost certainly desert him.

Secondly, if the Qur'an stated anything running counter to the known facts of his life and character, his credit would have been irretrievably compromised and his mission would have ended in failure, as his enemies, the unbelieving desert Arabs, were ever ready to discredit him in all possible ways. Hence, when the Qur'an states, for instance, that prior to his receipt of the revelation he did not entertain any aspiration nor made any preparation for playing the part of a Prophet, or that he did not read any book, and was an "unlettered" person, that information is to be accepted as absolutely correct. For, otherwise, he would have been instantly contradicted and held up to ridicule and discredit by his own people who knew him intimately since his boyhood. Hence, besides the divine origin of the Qur'an, this absolute contemporaneity it's self invests it with a peculiar authenticity.[6]

---

5.   Qur'an, 41: 41-42.
6.   Ali, *Sirat Al-Nabi*, 4-7.

Divine revelations are messages of God to mankind sent down through prophets. Revelations give a detailed description of the qualities, and attributes of God in whom man is required to believe and whom he is required to serve and worship. In addition, divine revelations also contain the code of life on which depends people's well being in this life. Some of the existing revealed books are the *Torah* (The Pentateuch, or the first five books of the old Testament), which was revealed to Musa (Moses); *Zabur* (Psalms), revealed to Da 'ud (David); *Injil* (the New Testament), revealed to Isa (Jesus); and finally the Qur'an, revealed to Muhammad (peace be upon him and on all other Prophets). Regarding the fact that God is the source of all love, the Prophet of Islam, Muhammad (p.b.u.h)[7] said: "Verily, God had created one hundred (types) of mercies, and has used only one (out of the whole lot) to distribute amongst his creatures. He has preserved the remaining ninety-nine until the Day of Judgement."[8] Therefore, the existence of intimacy and friendship amongst human beings and that amongst animals or other creatures are all due to the mercy of God. That sort of love that binds members of the opposite sex together is from the mercy of God. The fountainhead of love is God. Without the mercy of God, there would not have been any love, there wouldn't have been any affection between mankind; yet still, there wouldn't have been that tender-heartedness and mutual affection that envelops married couples and their offspring.

The Love of God takes Precedence

Love is a divine gift that God has implanted between His servants, so that with it, they will seek His pleasure and hope for His mercy and forgiveness on the Day of Judgement. It's imperative that all lovers who have Faith conduct their romantic relationships in accordance with what has been ordained by God, not as they wish, and in accordance with the teachings of Muhammad, the messenger of God, not as their whims and caprices dictate. The fact that, God, is the fountainhead of all love, our Sustainer and Nourisher, our relationship and love for Him should take precedence over our relationship with, and love for one another. But how do we love God? God demands that man should worship Him alone, not associate anything with Him, and obey Him by following the guidance he has received from Him through His prophets.

---

7.   "Peace be upon him" is subsequently shortened to (p.b.u.h).
8.   Related by *Al Bukhari* in his authentic collections of the traditions of the Prophet.

It may be pointed out at this juncture that by nature man is a follower and worshipper. If he is not devoted to God, he will devote himself to others: Hollywood stars, musicians, deities, saints, thinkers, philosophers or even national heroes in the like of Dr. Sun Yat-sen—the father of Modern China; Osagyefo Dr. Kwame Nkrumah of Ghana—the Champion of African Unity; Nikolai Lenin—leader of the Bolshevik Revolution in Russia, and father of the former Soviet Union; Sir Winston Churchill–British war–time Prime Minister; George Washington—first President of the United States of America; Karl Marx–father of Marxism or even Adolf Hitler—father of Nazism—following them in thought and action. And they, being human like himself (or worse in the case of deities), will lead him no where. In fact they needed guidance themselves, although, they may have been too high and mighty to accept it.

According to Islam, the love of God should be incumbent upon the love of His servant and Messenger Muhammad (peace be upon him). Islam has therefore equated the love of Muhammad to the love of God. But how do we love Muhammad if we have never met or seen him? It's by simply obeying his teachings and instructions. The Holy Qur'an says:

> "Say (Muhammad):
> If ye do love Allah,
> Follow me: Allah will love you
> And forgive you your sins
> For Allah is oft-Forgiving,
> Most Merciful."[9]

From an Islamic perspective, the love of God and his messenger, Muhammad, must be the highest attainment people involved in a romantic relationship should strive for. The love of God and his messenger therefore, should be above all love. The Holy Qur'an says:

> "Say (Muhammad):
>
> If it be that your fathers,
> Your sons, your brothers,
> Your mates or your kindred:
> The wealth that ye have gained;

---

9.   Qur'an, 3:31.

The commerce in which ye fear
A decline: or the dwellings
In which ye delight
Are dearer to you than Allah
Or His Messenger, the striving
In His cause; wait
Until Allah brings about
His decision: and Allah
Guides not the rebellious."[10]

Man's heart clings to (1) his own kith and kin—parents, children, brothers and sisters, husbands or wives, or other relatives (2) wealth and prosperity, (3) commerce or means of profit or gain, or (4) noble buildings, for dignity or comfort. If these are a hindrance in the obedience of God, we have to choose which we love most. We must love God even if it involves the sacrifice of all else. If we love our earthly ties and comforts, profit's and pleasures, more than we love God, and therefore, fail to respond to God's cause, it is not God's cause that will suffer. God's purpose will be accomplished, with or without us. But our failure to respond to His will must leave us bereft of grace and guidance: "for God guides not the rebellious".

But the love of God does not occur in a vacuum. It comes about due to a keen observation and reflection of the creation around and above us. A vivid reminder in the Holy Qur'an is:

"Do they not look
At the camels,
How they are made?
And at the Sky,
How it is raised?
And at the mountains,
How they are fixed firm?
And at the Earth,
How it is spread out?"[11]

---

10.   Qur'an, 9:24.
11.   Qur'an, 88:17-21.

The love of God is not blind love. It's a divine love and therefore in case man neglects his love for God or refuses to recognize His existence, he is asked to contemplate four things, which he can see in every-day life, and which are full of meaning, superb design and the goodness of God to man. We've got to have a reason to love God. The first mentioned is the domesticated animal, which for Arabs living in the desert is the camel. What a wonderful structure has this Ship of the Desert? He can store water in his stomach for days. He can live on dry and thorny desert shrubs. His limbs are adapted to his life. He can carry men and goods. His flesh can be eaten. Camel's hair can be used in weaving. Above all, he is so gentle.

The second thing man is called attention to, is the noble blue vault high above us—that contains the sun and the moon, the stars and the planets, and other heavenly bodies. This scene is full of beauty and magnificence; design and order; plainness and mystery. And yet we receive our light and warmth from the sun, and what would our physical lives be without these influences that come from such enormous distances? From every-day utility and affection in the camel, to the utility and grandeur in the heavens above us, we had two instances touching our individual as well as our social lives. In the third instance, in the Mountains we come to the utility to human kind generally in the services the Mountains perform in storing water in moderating climate, and in various other ways which is the business of Physical Geography to investigate and describe. The fourth and last instance given is that of the Earth as a whole, the habitation of mankind. The Earth is a globe, and yet how marvelously it seems to be spread out before us in plains, valleys, hills, deserts, seas, etc! Can man, seeing all these, fail to see a plan and purpose in his life? Fail to love God and turn to this great Creator? But the love of God also entails being God–conscious at all times.

"Men who remember Allah
Standing, sitting,
And lying down on their sides,
And contemplate
The (wonders of) creation
In the heavens and the earth,
(With the saying):
'Our Lord not for naught
Hast Thou created (all) this!
Glory to thee! Give us

Salvation from the Chastisement
Of the Fire.""[12]

Isn't it true that a true lover would always love to keep in close contact with his or her sweetheart? A true lover of God would at all times put God in mind in all his or her romantic relationships.

God has praised true lovers (of Him) in the Holy Qur'an as follows:

"Yet there are men
Who take (for worship)
Others besides Allah,
As equal with (with Allah):
They love them
As they should love Allah.
But those of Faith are
Overflowing in their love
For Allah…"[13]

Yes, if man's love for God is sincere and intense, so will be his love for his "significant other". And the more man keeps remembering God, the more he will keep thinking about his sweetheart, even if they are living thousands of miles apart. He would remain loyal to his "First Lady", there wouldn't be room for infidelity. Thus all romantic relationships in Islam are based upon our individual relationships with God. If your relationship with God is perfect, your relationship with your lover will also be perfect. The Muslim's love for God does not contradict his love for his wife and children, so far as this love (for one's wife and children) is in consonance with, not in opposition to, or a hindrance to one's love for God.

The reason why Islam has required that lovers first of all love God above all other things is a means of purification for the heart. When the love of God settles in the heart of a true believer, it cleanses the heart—the seat of all passion—from all impurities. The love for God negates greediness, pride, dishonesty, discrimination and racial superiority from the heart. There is no amount of chemotherapy, or heart surgery that is capable of cleansing the heart from the impurities men-

12.   Qur'an, 2:191.
13.   Qur'an, 2:165.

tioned above. God describes those who do not love and obey Him in the Holy Qur'an as:

> "In their hearts is a disease
> And Allah has increased
> Their disease…"[14]

The insincere lover who thinks he can get the best of both worlds by resorting to artful quibbling to obtain an advantage in a romantic relationship only increases the disease of his heart, because he is not true to himself. The Messenger of God, Muhammad (p.b.u.h) made a famous saying fourteen centuries ago when he said: "…verily, in the body there is a morsel of flesh which, if it be righteous, all the body is righteous and which if it be diseased, all of it is diseased. Truly it is the heart."[15] This morsel of flesh is the heart—the seat of every romantic relationship. Naturally, no one would like to sit on a seat that has not been properly cleaned, because he would get his clothes dirty. True love would only settle in that morsel of flesh that has been purified by the love of God. Therefore, when this writer says God is the source of every love this is what it means—at least from the Islamic perspective.

True Love and Paganism

There are others who although, are outside the pale of any religion, are true lovers. Like "Mr. Lee", he or she could argue that even though: "I am an atheist, and even don't believe in ancestor worship, I consider my self a true lover. I will not cheat on my girl friend or wife. I equally love my offspring. Then why do you say God is the source of all love, and that it's only the love of God that will purify my heart?" Some Africans who do not believe in either Christianity or Islam like "Mr. Chinedu" argue that Christianity and Islam are alien religions to Africans. "The White men (those slave traders), brought Christianity to colonize and subdue us; whereas Islam, brought to us by those desert Arabs should belong to them only, these two religions should have no place in black Africa…these religions have come to divide we Africans, just cast a glance at the civil war in Sudan and in some parts of Africa…the White man or Arab will only respect we Africans if we go back to our own roots and practice our own religion—Traditional African

---

14.   Qur'an, 2: 10.
15.   Related by *Al-Bukhari* and *Muslim*.

religion." "This is what our ancestors practiced—the best for we Africans." Chinedu asserted.

He then went on rumbling: "I will not cheat on my wife or girl friend. And if I fall in love, I shall remain faithful to my lover. I also oppose same-sex love and same-sex marriages—those Western notions of sexuality that threatens to pervert we Africans and turn our Continent upside down. Chinedu then attacked this writer: "So you this writer what are you talking about when you claim that, 'I'm not a true lover because I don't believe in your God of Islam?'" "Hold your fire!" This writer, in trying to appease his African brother said: "Nedu (a short form of Chinedu), please don't misunderstand me, I am not saying you can't be a true lover if you believe in Traditional African religion that entails ancestor worship and some lesser gods." "This writer insisted".

This writer's answer to his friend, Mr. Lee, was that: "Your not believing in the existence of God doesn't mean there is no God at all. Secondly, there are a lot of people who, despite their claim to be men of God aren't true lovers. It doesn't therefore mean that belief in God is tantamount to true love in any romantic relationship." This writer continued: "Mr. Lee, I understand some Asians like you (both old and young) still have the age old belief of spirit possession, and destinies written in the stars; and I am aware that some Koreans also believe the Universe is ruled by the interrelationship between fire, water, wood, metal and earth. Who created all these?" This writer asked Mr. Lee calmly. "Do you have a complete control over all your affairs in this world?" "Why is it that there are certain times you wished things that happened shouldn't have happened anyway?" "Can you prevent yourself from falling ill or dying?" "Your being a true lover is a trait bestowed upon you from someone you don't believe in, or love." "He is God." This writer concluded. His answer to Nedu who believes in Traditional African religion was similar to the one above. My African brother is worshipping ancestors who are long gone—they could not even prevent themselves from falling ill or dying. He is worshipping something someone molded with his own hands that could be devoured by fire; carried away by torrential rains; or annihilated during powerful earthquakes. Lee and Nedu should be reminded that, even though they do not believe in God, they still believe in something they might not be aware of—culture.

There is a well-known Chinese saying that: *Ru-jing sui-su or Ru- jing wen-su*, which could be literally translated as: "When you enter into a new environment, follow or ask about it's customs.". It's now generally translated as: "When in Rome do as the Romans do." If culture is construed as our shared consciousness; our common experience; the small things we all know; the characters in our stories; the morals those stories carry, then culture is what we absorb as we grow up; what we see and hear so often that we call it reality. Out of culture comes behavior. A people's culture is also derived from land, tools, materials, family, neighbors and nature. In most parts of the world, cultural leanings are more powerful than religious leanings. It's for this reason that my friends, Messrs Lee and Chinedu consider themselves to be true lovers. They think they would never cheat on their "significant halves", but how realistic are they? Since they don't believe in any accountability after death, there will be no any hindrance if they want to cheat on their partners—provided they will not be caught. Whereas a person who believes in God knows that he will be accountable to his Lord if he fools around.

At this point, it's better to note that religion and culture are antithesis of each other. Whereas religion, like Islam is universal, culture is indigenous to a particular area or region. Whenever cultural beliefs clashed with religious beliefs, the former always took precedence. There exist a vivid example in the Holy Qur'an where, in accordance with custom, a man inherited widows of his dead father—not necessarily because he loved them, but because of culture.

> "And marry not women
> Whom your fathers married,
> Except what is passed:
> It was shameful and odious,
> An abominable custom indeed."[16]

Among many nations, including Arabs in the pre-Islamic era, a step son or brother took possession of a dead man's widow or widows along with his chattels. This shameful custom had to be excoriated and forbidden. Women were inherited without their permission; men also inherited them because it was customary—not because of love. Some aspects of every culture known to man needed to be abolished or modified by some conquering forces or by divine guidance. For instance, the conquering Spaniards had to extirpate the practice of human sacrifice from Aztec culture. There is an old Chinese saying that: "If you don't beat up your wife every 3 days, she will start tearing up the roof tiles." It means that a wife not beaten is a wife out of control. This could illustrate a general idea that is holding sway among some men in every continent, so much so that it could even be mistaken (by them) to be a custom. Domestic violence is not indigenous to any particular region, race, color, or creed. "How does he says he loves me when

---

16. Qur'an, 4: 22.

he chases me up and down the stairs with a baseball bat; punches me on the face; throws the dishes at me?" A woman complained about her live-in boyfriend.

The love that exists between husbands and wives or that between a married couple and their offspring is innate, it's emotional and springs forth from the heart. The Messenger of God, Muhammad (p.b.u.h.), used to hug the children of his only surviving and beloved daughter, Fatima. One day, he came out of the house hugging one of them saying: "You (children) are the cause of niggardliness, cowardice and ignorance of your parents, due to your influence (on them), but certainly, you are a pleasant gift from God."[17] The meaning is that, a person's love for his children could make him become so intoxicated as to become mean, coward and ignorant. For instance, the coercive "one family, one child" legislation in China has inadvertently turned children there into "little Emperors". Modern wealth and doting parents have created an unruly brood of brats. The high suicide rate among Asian students seem not from pressure to study hard or do well at school, but from the young people's weakness in facing up to pressure—a characteristic of a society that prizes material well-being and slights spiritual values. The growing number of one child families in some parts of Asia will only create more "little Emperors". Parents then will become 'cowards' in the eyes of their children, more importantly, teachers who are supposed to educate future generations also will become 'cowards' in training the young ones—simply because the law says "Thou Shalt not Touch thy Child or Pupil." There are now some teachers who are becoming afraid to mete out even the slightest corrective punishment to their pupils, for the fear of being branded as "Child Abusers". This saying of the Prophet of Islam could not have been more intelligible during his lifetime 14 hundred years ago. It's meaning will become more vivid with an ever increasing number of "little Emperors" across Asia and beyond.

It's therefore noteworthy for lovers with Faith to understand that the foundation of their love, that is built upon honesty and purity, and their love for their offspring, that is built upon tenderness and compassion, does not contradict their love for God. On the contrary, their love for each other is a concomitant of their love of God. A true Muslim should be a lover of God and His Messenger; Muhammad (p.b.u.h.); a lover of his wife and offspring; a lover of all other people who do not persecute him due to his faith or religion. The Holy Qur'an says:

"Allah forbids you not,
With regards to those who

---

17.   Qanbas, *Al-Hubb Fil-Islam*, 24.

Fight you not for (your) Faith
Nor drive you out of your
Homes, from dealing kindly and
Justly with them:
For Allah loves those who are just."[18]

This means that Muslims should deal kindly and equitably, as is shown by the Prophet's own example, with non-Muslims—unless they are rampant and out to destroy them and their Faith.

The problem of falling birthrates is common to many developed countries, and this trend is not confined to Western countries alone, indeed, Hong Kong and Macao have the lowest birthrates in the world and are followed not far behind by Taiwan and Singapore. Statistics in Taiwan indicate that, 20 years ago, a woman could be expected to give birth to 2.8 children. In 2003, the rate dipped to 1.2 children.[19] Is the world not bracing it's self for more "little Emperors"? Late marriages and late pregnancies, according to *The China Post* have had an impact on the birthrate in Taiwan. An aging population is a common problem seen in developed countries too.

A Taiwanese official in charge of Health said that, as part of it's efforts to slow down the trend, the Bureau of Health encourages women to get married before the age of 30 and conceive before the age of 35. But women do not get married in a vacuum, if they would marry at all, they need to marry men with true love, and if they are not sure about these men, they are never going to get married. The underlying problem is how to make the world safe for true love. It is a man's world, and women are not going to get married just because they want to have children.

---

18. Qur'an, 60:18.
19. *China Post*, (Taipei), 20 August 2004.

4

SCALING THE MOUNTAIN OF LOVE[1]

There is no any human being on earth unless he or she has a heart that throbs and two eyes that see. The human heart doesn't become devoid of the yearning for love, nor does it become devoid of an atom of sympathy and mercy. But it's the usage of these yearnings that matters. They could be directed toward corrupting the society or reforming it. There is no doubt that every young man or woman might have had a romantic relationship with the opposite sex—it might have been real or imagined. However, there is no need to compile a dictionary of relationships between men and women, their successes and failures. What is intended here is a survey of these relationships, the extent to which they can proceed, and how they should end in the eyes of Islam. The first most important thing to take note of in resolving problems associated with relationships is the saying of the Prophet of Islam: "We have not seen anything better for lovers other than marriage."[2] Every romantic relationship is considered to be deficient if it's not crowned with marriage. Every love is considered fake unless authenticated by marriage.

Getting Started

When Edmund Hillary and Sherpa Tenzing became the world's first climbers to conquer Mount Everest (the world's highest peak), they became instant heroes. In a like manner, lovers who are able to conquer the Mountain of Love become heroes. Marriage is what one finds at the summit of the Love Mountain. The Love Mountain could be a very high one to climb, it could also be a very low one;

---

1. Used in a figurative sense.
2. Related by *Ibn Majah* in his authentic collections of the Prophets traditions.

46

depending on the partners involved. Other partners might even decide that they do not wish to scale to the top of this peak—thus being content only by hanging around it's edges, and making love to each other. The Love Mountain could be scaled at any time in a person's lifetime. Others might decide to scale it during the 'spring' of their lives; bearing in mind that spring is a green season and the Love Mountain is yet green; others might think it would be better to scale it in the 'summer' of their lives. Summer is a blue season; the sky is blue; it is hot in summer; one would have to be better prepared to climb the Love Mountain during this period of one's life. Yet still, some people might also see it appropriate to scale it in the 'fall' or 'winter' of their lives. As we all know, Fall is a yellow season, and leaves are all yellow during this season. Those about to scale this Mountain during this period of their lives might have already gone through their mid-life crisis. Winter is a white season; it is freezing in winter, and those planning to scale this Mountain might have realized they might not possess enough energy to do so without some doses of Viagra (if they are men). To this writer, the 'Spring' of one's life is between the ages of 18 and 30. The 'Summer' of one's life is between the ages 31 and 40. That of 'Fall' is between the ages 41 and 63; whereas that of 'Winter' starts from age 63 onwards. It would be arduous and unspeakably exhaustive to scale this Mountain after age 63. The above categorization has not been done arbitrarily. The writer has taken into consideration certain aspects of The Prophet's life. Muhammad (p.bu.h) got married at the age of 25; considered by this writer to be the 'Spring' of his life. He received his first revelation, and attained Prophethood at the age of 40; considered by this writer to be the 'Summer' of his life. He died at the age of 63; considered by this writer to be the 'Fall' of his life.

Some clues concerning this categorization can be found in the Holy Qur'an:

> "…At length, when he reaches
>
> The age of full strength and attains
>
> Forty years…"[3]

The age of full strength is termed *ashudd* in the Qur'an; it falls between 18 and 30 or 32. Between 30 and 40 a man is said to be in his best manhood. After 40, he begins to look after his growing children; perhaps his spiritual faculties also gain the upper hand after 40. When mid-life crisis begins to set in, a man

---

3.   Qur'an, 46: 15.

could be conveniently said to be 'creeping' toward the 'Fall' of his life. Then the cold season sets in with it's freezing temperatures; a person at this age, will be said to have passed the age of 63. However, in some parts of the world (especially sub-Saharan Africa), where life expectancy at birth is below 55 years,[4] how many men (and women) would live long enough to scale the Mountain of Love during the 'Fall' of their lives? No matter what time in life a person decides to undertake the risky business of climbing the Mountain of Love, some preparations are inevitable, for the climbing could take a very long time, it could be arduous and the path, tortuous.

In scaling the Mountain of Love, it's better to have a congenial companion. When Abu Bakr and Umar, (both companions) of the Prophet, who later succeeded him as the first and second Caliphs of Islam respectively; proposed to marry his daughter, Fatimah, the Prophet declined and said: "She is a small girl." But when Ali, the Prophet's cousin, who later became the fourth Caliph of Islam; proposed marriage to Fatima, his request was accepted and they were subsequently married.[5] The Prophet's refusal to marry his beloved daughter, Fatima, to either Abu Bakr or Umar wasn't because they were not God-fearing enough, or that they had some unspecified physical defects. Rather, it was due to their age. Fatima was close to 40 years younger than both men. On the other hand, Ali, the Prophet's cousin was within an accepted age limit. This was meant to provide a lesson to Muslims who would like to force their younger daughters to marry older men for the sake of money, prestige or whatever reasons. In Islam the Mountain of Love is to be climbed voluntarily; not by coercion, and by that love that is mutual; not lop-sided.

In order that the climbing of this Mountain take place in a very conducive ambience, Islam has made it compulsory that prospective 'climbers' first of all meet with each other, and get to know each other. So that, it does not happen that, after climbing halfway, one partner begins to snap at the other's ankles. After a man from the *Ansars.*[6] proposed to a woman and informed the Prophet about it, he asked: "Did you look at her?" His answer was an emphatic "No." The Prophet then said: "Go and look at her, surely there is something in the eyes of the *Ansars.*" The Prophet also said to Mugheera, the son of Shu'ba (one of his companions), who informed him of his proposal to a certain woman, "Go and

---

4.   John L. Allen, *Student Atlas of World Politics*, 3rd ed., (Guilford: Dushkin/McGraw Hill, 1998), 64.
5.   Al-Sayyid Sabiq, *Fiqh Al-Sunnah*, vol.2 (in Arabic) (Beirut: Dar Al-Fikr, 1983), 19.
6.   *Ansars,* translated literally as the "Helpers" were the people of Madina who welcomed the Prophet Muhammad (p.b.u.h) to their city after his Hegira from Mecca.

look at her, for it's likely that (through your looking at each other), the feeling of affection and companionship would occur between you."[7] At the time both partners are looking at each other, and their eyes meeting each other, their body chemistry eventually causes them to fall in love. At this time, the man would see through the eyes of his future wife, that radiation of ethereal beauty; the woman would also see through the eyes of her future husband, those sweet smiles of his that are genuine, rather than cloying. However, the meeting between both must not occur in a secluded place, or without a chaperon or a relative.

The best guide in climbing the Mountain of Love is God-consciousness and trust in Him. Because with God-consciousness, lovers would know the secure path to take so as to avoid unwanted outcomes. With their trust in God, they would be able to endure the hardships associated with scaling this treacherous Mountain. They would continue to pray that God deliver them safely. They would definitely encounter all aspects of lovers on their way to the top. And anytime, they stumble, and fall down; they would quickly get up; gather more momentum; and keep up the fight. It would only be the potency of faith and prayer that would lead them to the summit. Their prayers would be:

> "Our Lord! Bestow on us
> Mercy from Thyself,
> And dispose of our affair
> For us in the right way!"[8]

Besides being mindful of, and putting their trust in God, young lovers need their parents as 'Sherpa guides' too. They will always be available to provide the necessary assistance to them as they embark upon the journey up the Love Mountain. And, although, parents have no right to put their children through forced marriages, their relevance at this juncture cannot be over-emphasized. They are experienced 'climbers'; they have gotten to the top of the Love Mountain already—and have gotten married. Therefore they are capable of steering young lovers through to the summit—avoiding all the pitfalls all the way to the top. The Holy Qur'an attaches great importance to filial piety in these words:

---

7.   Sabiq, *Fiqh Al-Sunnah*, 19.
8.   Qur'an, 18:10.

"Thy Lord hath decreed
That ye worship none but Him,
And that ye be kind to parents.
Whether one or both of them
Attain old age in thy life-time,
Say not to them a word of contempt,
Nor repel them, address them,
In terms of honor. And out of kindness,
Lower to them the wing of humility,
And say: 'My Lord bestow on them
Thy mercy even as they cherished me
In childhood.'"[9]

The spiritual and moral duties of lovers are hereby brought into juxtaposition. In Islam one is expected to love God, and also love his or her parents. We are to worship none but God, because none but God is worthy of worship, not because "the Lord thy God is a jealous God, visiting the iniquity of the fathers upon the children unto the third and fourth generation of them that hate Me" (Exod. xx. 5). "Lower to them the wing of humility," this metaphor is that of a high-flying bird which lowers her wing out of tenderness to her offspring. There is a double aptness. When the parent was strong, and the child helpless, parental affection was showered on the child: When the child grows up and is strong, and the parent is helpless, can he or she do less than bestow similar tender care on the parent? More than this: He or she must approach the matter with gentle humility: for does not parental love, remind him or her of the great love with which God—the source of all love—cherishes His creatures?

It's customary to make provisions for a journey, no matter where the journey takes one to, whether to the land of birds, the land of insects, snails or porcupines. It indeed does not matter if the journey is taking one to the land of the dead. Nature demands of every traveler to make provisions for every journey. Therefore, it's recommended that every lover make sufficient provision for his or her journey up the Love Mountain. As usual, the Holy Qur'an advises believers embarking upon a journey as follows:

---

9.   Qur'an, 17:23-24.

"…And take a provision
(With you) for the journey,
But the best of provisions
Is right conduct.
So fear Me, O ye that are wise."[10]

In taking any journey on earth, the thoughts of the Muslim is at once directed from the physical to the spiritual. The best of such provisions as mentioned in the Qur'an is right conduct, which is the same as the fear of God. Undoubtedly, the fear of God is the beginning of wisdom. Thus in attempting to climb up the Mountain of Love, the best provision from the Islamic viewpoint is the fear of God. If both partners in a romantic relationship choose to make the fear of God their best provision for their journey, this journey wouldn't be only short; it would be made easier and less arduous. In this regard, teen-age pregnancies; sexually transmitted diseases (STDs); guilt and pain; would not become terrible exchanges for few stolen moments. By employing the fear of God as the best provision, Islam seeks to slam the door in the face of any partner involved in a romantic relationship, whose only intention is climbing this Mountain just for pleasure; without any real matrimonial intention.

The Safest Passage

Islam has also laid down a safe passage through which lovers should take during their journey up the Love Mountain. This passage isn't serpentine, it's straight and short. This is meant to protect climbers from falling into pitfalls. Therefore, it's imperative that, once the aura of love begins to make rounds between two people belonging to the opposite sex, there is the urgent need to effect a marriage contract. There is no need to waste time or indulge oneself in re-examining the relationship over and over. The reason is that at this moment, it's only the heart that is supposed to take charge not the head. A man might say: "I do not know this girl very well, and she doesn't also know me well too, I intend to get more acquainted with her habit's and her lifestyle. I wish to befriend her for a while!" A girl in love might also delay marriage for similar reasons.

In traveling between the foot of the Love Mountain, and it's top, where marriage is to be found, lovers might decide to use the time interval to befriend each other and get to know each other better. But there is a risk in doing that. What

---

10.   Qur'an, 2:197

of, if after climbing half-way one partner decides that the other partner is no longer suitable for the journey and decides to abandon him or her there and then? Why should you choose to abandon your partner mid-way after he or she has already made up his or her mind to be with you forever, and hopes to realize them by your side? If you decide to abandon him or her half way the Mountain, aren't you exposing him or her to fall prey to other "creatures"? Would any brother accept such a treatment for his sister? And would any sister accept such a treatment for her brother? In today's Information Age, how many engaged couples have abandoned one another mid-way up the Love Mountain just for one reason or another? They have been left hanging halfway on the Love Mountain. Some have in effect turned into "shrub roses"[11] scattered along the edges of the Love Mountain.

This has resulted in many men and women committing suicide or attempting to commit suicide. Recently, a Taiwanese woman threatened to commit suicide on two occasions in an attempt to get her boyfriend marry her. "I won't feel secure unless I get married." She was heard saying. Firefighters and police had to bring her boyfriend to the scene along with an empty marriage certificate. The woman then asked the police to be witnesses for the makeshift wedding. The officers had to say yes to prevent a tragedy.[12] Those who do not commit suicide suffer from depression, some become demented, indeed, others are often confounded and are at a lost as to how to fall out of love. To some people, falling in love is often much easier than falling out of love! These have been some of the problems associated with unfulfilled romantic relationships. It has often been due to the loss of trust between lovers. Nowadays, it's often an uphill battle to maintain a true and loving relationship in such a hostile and ungodly environment as we find ourselves. There are now a whole lot of Internet chat rooms, that have created a new generation of "e-lovers". The result has been that, most lovers are no longer secure. The Love Mountain has now been festooned with so many "creatures" who are ready to snatch away other people's partners. For the above reasons, Islam has made God-consciousness the most important asset of a person involved in a romantic relationship. In a romantic relationship, if God consciousness is the rule of the game, even series of unhappy relationships would finally end with the nirvana of a perfect marriage.

---

11.   "Shrub roses"—a term employed by this writer to denote men and women whose dreams of marrying their partners have been shattered due to no fault of theirs.
12.   *China Post* (Taipei), 17 May 2004.

As a matter of principle, the Prophet of Islam advises lovers planning to climb up the Mountain of Love in the following words: "Beware of the attractive green foliage that grows out of manure made from animal excrement." Then his companions asked: "What is meant by 'the attractive green foliage that grows out of manure made from animal excrement, O the Prophet of God?'" The Prophet then said: "It's a beautiful woman who has been raised in a bad home."[13] This could be said of a man too. Should a young man or woman decide to climb the Mountain of Love with such a person who is bad mannered, how far will they be able to go up the Love Mountain? How steadfast would such a bad-mannered partner be, during their journey up this Mountain surrounded by twists and turns? Unfortunately, this has been what we are now witnessing in the Information Age; young men now hanker after beautiful women—forgetting that beauty is only skin deep. Young women also now hanker after wealth.

The type of true love that is supposed to lead lovers toward the Mountain top (marriage), has fallen in standards, it has indeed hit it's lowest level whereby a lover is only interested in hankering after materialism and carnal desires. In such a manner, fake lovers are now putting on a veneer of piety and respectability in order to hypnotize others in search of true love. Their masquerading as true lovers is soon exposed, once they achieve their aims. In our search for true lovers, the Prophet of Islam teaches us a safer method of how to go about that by saying: "A woman is to be married based on four factors; due to her wealth, her pedigree, her beauty, or due to her religiosity, but it's better to select the religious one, by so doing, may your hands become smeared with earth."[14] The last phrase of this saying, "may your hands become smeared with earth," is an expression of affection; other scholars interpret it as "an expression wishing poverty to befall a person who marries a woman for some other reasons other than due to her piety."[15] It's most likely that one finds a partner possessing two or three of these qualities—religion, pedigree and good looks. In a world that so idolizes outer beauty—that is fated to fade in time, it's essential that Islam draw our attention to the only beauty that really lasts—inner beauty.

This writer is keenly aware that people who dwell so much on religion are usually considered old-fashioned in today's world. Despite this, a survey of people's religious beliefs carried out in 10 countries in January 2004, suggested religion was still holding sway in some countries of the world. Over 90 percent of Nigeri-

---

13.   Related by *Al-Dar Qutniyyi* in his collections of the Prophetic traditions.
14.   Related by *Al-Bukhari* and *Muslim* in their authentic collections of the Prophetic traditions.
15.   Sabiq, *Fiqh Al-Sunnah* (in Arabic), 17.

ans said they believed in God, prayed regularly and would die for their belief. The highest levels of belief were found in the world's poorest countries, as well as the United States. India and Indonesia were also recorded as countries with a high level of belief in God. In most of the countries covered, well over 80 percent said they believed in God or a higher power. In Nigeria, the figure was 100 percent, and in the US 91 percent, with the United Kingdom scoring lowest at 67 percent. In most countries, 80 percent of the sample agreed that a belief in God or a higher power made people better human beings.[16]

Islam is not an exclusive religion. Social intercourse, including inter-marriage, is permissible with *Ahlul Kitaab* (People of The Book), a term used in the Qur'an to denote Christians and Jews. Although there are doctrinal differences in the Oneness of God, and of Prophethood, these two religions, including Islam, are known as the three monotheistic religions. A Muslim may choose a woman from their ranks to climb the Mountain of Love with; he may do that on the same terms as he would with a Muslim woman; he must give her an economic and moral status, and must not be actuated merely by motives of lust or physical desire. A Muslim woman may not climb this Mountain with a non-Muslim man, because her Muslim status would be affected; the wife ordinarily takes the nationality and status given by her husband's law. Any man or woman of any race or faith, may, on accepting Islam, freely climb the Mountain of Love with any Muslim woman or man, provided it is from motives of purity and chastity and not lewdness. God Almighty says about their marriage by Muslims in the Qur'an as follows:

> "…Lawful unto you in marriage
> Are (not only) chaste women who
> Are believers, but chaste women
> From the People of the Book revealed
> Before your time; when ye give them
> Their due dowers, and desire chastity,
> Not lewdness. Taking them as lovers…"[17]

---

16. *BBC Program, What The World Thinks About God,*. ICM poll [news on-line]; accessed 26 February 2004, available from http://news.bbc.co.uk/2/hi/programmes/wtwtgod/3490490.stm; internet.

17. Qur'an, 5:5.

Potential lovers have become more sophisticated in their choice of partners. It pays to be choosy though. But is it true that people who refuse to accept anything but the best often get it? In terms of romance, who is to be considered the 'best' partner? The one capable of "heating up" the marital bed, the best and the brightest, the one with good looks, the wealthiest, the kind-hearted, the President's daughter or son, or simply the one you happen to fall in love with? These are questions that may annoy the daylight out of every single male or female aspiring to go hiking on the Mountain of Love. A Japanese lady recently complained: "Years ago, when you reached a certain age, relatives—without asking—would bring a partner, today, people are freer, but the process of finding someone isn't easy."

In his letter to an advice column, one American man wrote: "…I'm at the end of my tether and not sure what to do. Basically, my question is, what exactly is it that women in my generation are looking for? I'm a 23 year-old law student and political activist who also loves ballroom, dancing and classical music. Everyone tells me I'm a great listener and I put other people first. After all this, not only have I had a date in years, but also women don't even give me a second look. When I asked my women friends, they tell me that any woman would be lucky to have me…but no one is interested. Any idea of what I might be missing to make my generation swoon?" He signed off as—Lovesick Legal Eagle. The answer given to this "LLE" was even more interesting.

"Different women look for different things, my friend. Among them: kindness, humor, looks, money, smarts, status, knowledge, big sex drive, no sex drive, large family, no family, lovely friends, good taste, a yacht, ability to listen, the gift of gab, multiple degrees, ambition…I will spare you the laundry list. What women find appealing is determined by needs, neurosis and background…"[18] It's, therefore, safe to conclude that people now use logic not their hearts in choosing a partner. But why is the divorce rate world-wide on the rise? It may be that, lovers have become incapable of "spicing up" their love lives. Divorce then becomes the only recourse.

Islam attaches great importance to the way and manner a person should choose a partner who would climb the Mountain of Love with him or her. In Islam the first priority is the religiosity of the other partner, then of course comes other preferences that a lover might want to see in the other partner. With religiosity comes the fear of God. A man came to Hasan, the grandson of the Prophet of Islam Muhammad (p.b.u.h.) and asked: "I have a daughter. Who should she

---

18. *China Post*, (Taipei) 7 May 2004.

be betrothed to?" Hasan replied: "She should be betrothed to a person who fears God; for if he loves her, he will treat her with magnanimity; and even if he doesn't love her that much, he would not oppress her."[19] As human beings, we are naturally inclined to love anything beautiful, sometimes a man would feel that he would not be totally happy if he is deprived of getting married to a particular beautiful woman. For this reason Islam has not kept quiet about a Muslim's right to marry beautiful women. The Prophet of Islam said: "Surely God is elegant, and He loves elegance."[20] Therefore, pulchritude in a woman is God's gift to man.

People who still believe love is blind are entitled to their ideas, however, this writer begs to differ. His reasons are that, when two lovers begin to trek up the Love Mountain, they are supposed to be guided by the love that exists between them. And as they go up higher, the more intense their love for each other grows. If this love is blind, how can they be able to avoid say, "landmines" and other "creatures" on their way to the top? How can a blind man climb a mountain without a guide? Any mountain climber needs to have a strong determination to get to the top of any mountain he or she is attempting to climb. In Islam, the basis of this determination should be religiosity (or God-consciousness), and a good disposition. A man or woman who is God-fearing and good mannered therefore, is not supposed to be denied marrying a woman of his or her choice because of the lack of wealth. Such a good and religious person could become mischievous and vicious if he or she is denied his or her choice of a lover.

In the light of this, so-called "honor killings", that claims hundreds of women's lives each year is not permitted in Islam. Although "honor killings" is illegal in Pakistan and other Islamic countries, hundreds of women are put to death by male members of their family every year for choosing a husband without their family's approval, or for having affairs. Most "honor killings" occur because young and unmarried girls are deflowered. There are laws in the Qur'an stipulating how to deal with Muslims who are guilty of sexual misconduct. It's only the Islamic court that has the right to impose judgment—not individuals. Ibn Abbas (one of the companions of the Prophet), reported that a girl came to the Messenger of God, Muhammad (p.b.u.h), and reported that her father had forced her to marry without her consent. The Messenger of God gave her the choice (between accepting the marriage or invalidating it). In another version, the girl said: Actually I accept this marriage but, I wanted to let women know that parents have no

19.   Sabiq, *Fiqh Al-Sunnah*, 20.
20.   Ibid., 19.

right to (force a husband on them).[21] However, it's necessary that in choosing a lover, attention must be paid to the differences in age, social standing, economic and educational levels.

Just as the woman has the right to choose who would climb the Mountain of Love with her, she also has the right to look at that partner and to make sure he does not possess any physical defects. It's her birthright to decide that an one-eyed man, a man with a limping leg, or a man suffering from an incurable disease would not climb the Mountain with her. Therefore in choosing a partner, Islam attaches great importance to both the spiritual and physical aspects of lovers. In scaling Mount Everest that is situated in Nepal, climbers need Sherpa guides to guide them through to the summit. The same thing happens in climbing the Love Mountain in Islam. Climbers need to be guided so as to avoid "landmines", and other dangerous "creatures". They are expected to follow designated paths, they are not often left alone to wander hither and thither on their way up. It is also recommended that they get to the summit as fast as they can. Their ambition should be to get to the top as soon as they can.

The Possible Dangers

In this information Age, the road up the Love Mountain has become over-crowded with "landmines"[22], the climbing has become tougher and dangerous; the road up this Mountain compares favorably with the "killing fields of Cambodia"; where more than 100, 000 landmines were planted by former warring factions; that resulted in at least 300 Cambodians loosing their hands and legs every month some years back. Islam advises lovers to tread up this Mountain with tactical flexibility, or else when they step on a "landmine", the earth under their feet will revolt, and then they get tossed into the air, they then fall down from the Mountain. By the time they get up to start again, they find their colleagues in true love already ahead of them in time and space. Nightmares and tears persist for some lovers who were unable to find true love. Their gullibility prevented them from being able to separate cheese from chalk; consequently, their regrets now hang heavily on their backs. Their present loveless lives; and their future resolve to find true and enduring love, offers only fleeting consolations.

---

21. Related by *Ibn Hanbal* and *Ibn Majah.*
22. "Landmines" employed by this writer denote the daunting logistics of life that might prevent men and women willing to get married from achieving their goal.

These days, it's not only finances that discourage people from getting married, but also the daunting logistics of life: the desire to have one's own home, a stable job, a luxurious automobile, and (in some societies), a Darwinian educational system. These are what this writer regards as the "landmines" that could threaten lovers as they scale the Love Mountain. At any 'season' of one's life, one would always find the Love Mountain over-crowded, with other 'climbers' when one embarks upon climbing this Mountain. They climb for different reasons. However, it's very difficult to know how many of these would finally make it to the top. There are others who might be climbing it just for fun. These climbers are not interested in getting to the top. They are content with hanging around the edges of this Mountain and having fun as long as they can. But the nights of enjoyment and pleasure will not continue forever!

Some of these "creatures" on the Love Mountain have a knack in carrying out a surreptitious search for gullible men or women scaling this Mountain. Yet still, there are those climbers who have been left stranded half way. These are those who said, "yes" to love too soon and "no" to sex too late. Least did they realize that their partners wanted them only as "usable and expendable commodities". In sub-Saharan Africa, where poverty is rife, young girls are often driven into prostitution in order to be able to fend for themselves and their families. They (sometimes) are saddled with the burden of having to deal with unwanted pregnancies or children engendered out of wedlock. These are the "shrub roses" of the Love Mountain. Let's be honest, what does a man loses if a woman dumps him? He can quickly get his acts together and start to date again. The same can't be said of a poor woman who often has to depend on some "creatures" for her livelihood. To be sure, a woman is more emotional, and being dumped by the man she loves may leave her with a never-ending rancor. How many are the objects of lessons for lovers, and how less is the taking of these lessons!

Islam, therefore appeals to lovers to be true and genuine lovers. In the midst of the darkness that engulfed the world, the divine revelation echoed in the wilderness of the Arabian Desert with a fresh, noble and universal message to humanity. God says in the Holy Qur'an:

> "O Mankind, keep your duty to your Lord,
> Who created you from a single soul and
> From it created it's mate (of same kind)
> And from them twain has spread a multitude

Of men and women; fear Allah, through

Whom ye demand your mutual (rights)

And be heedful of the wombs (that bore you)…"[23]

"From it" here refers to the kind—from the same kind, or of like nature, God created it's mate. A scholar who pondered about this verse states: "It is believed that there is no text, old or new, that deals with the humanity of the woman from all aspects with such amazing brevity, eloquence, depth and originality as this divine decree."[24]

Stressing this noble and natural conception, the Qur'an states further:

"It is He who created

You from a single soul,

And made his mate of

Like nature, in order

That he might dwell

With her (in love)…"[25]

That he might dwell in her in true love, not fake love, which could be deleterious to the individual and the society. The Prophet of Islam stated fourteen hundred years ago: "We have not seen anything better for lovers other than marriage."[26] In other words, one only finds 'marriage' at the zenith of the mountain of love.

In today's world, we may be smarter, more competitive, mobile, technologically savvy and adept at forming relationships, but we may not be all that smart at taking a good care of our parents. On the hand, how smart are we in climbing the Mountain of Love? In Islam young lovers are reminded to be God-conscious and to at least give their parents a chance to be their 'Sherpa guides' as they scale the Love Mountain. They are not to be left alone to wonder on the Mountain aimlessly—falling in and out of love several times in a year. We are asked to honor our father and mother, not "that thy days may be long upon the land which the

---

23. Qur'an, 4:1.
24. Jamal A. Badawi, *The Status of Women In Islam*, (Plainfield, Department of Education and Training, MSA of U.S. and Canada, 1980), 11.
25. Qur'an, 7:189.
26. Related by *Ibn Majah*.

Lord thy God giveth thee" (Exod.xx. 12), but upon much higher and more universal grounds such as befit a perfected revelation. In the first place, not merely respect, but cherishing kindness and humility to parents are commanded. In the second place the command is bracketed with the command to worship the One True God. Parental love should be to us a type of divine love: nothing that we can do can ever compensate for that which we have received. Then why do we choose to neglect them when we choose to scale the Love Mountain? They may be divorced, yes, but they have been there before at the top. Lets give them that credit!

At the foot of the Love Mountain is a marriage proposal, and at it's summit is marriage itself. Between marriage proposal and marriage it's self is the *Mahr*, a marriage gift, which is presented to the wife-to-be by her lover and is included in the nuptial contract. To be sure, the Love Mountain is as old and tired as the word "love" it's self.

5

BEING AT THE ZENITH OF THE LOVE MOUNTAIN

When two lovers have been able to climb up to the top of the Love Mountain, it's only natural that they would now like to tie the knot. Their love for each other would now be said to have attained a considerable degree of maturity and perfection. At this point, there could still be certain impediments capable of stopping these lovers from realizing their eternal desire to be together. In some parts of the world, especially in the Middle East, *Mahr*, or marriage gift could become such an impediment. *Mahr* in some Islamic countries continue to pose a serious threat to lovers—especially to the young men who wish to perfect their relationships through marriage. The amount of *Mahr* demanded in these countries has become backbreaking to lovers wanting to get married; it often turns the woman into a commodity on sale. What parents and guardians do forget is that; these two lovers have already reached the mountain-top of love, and if at this time a man is requested to pay a huge amount of *Mahr* to his wife-to-be, then love becomes meaningless.

The Problem with the Marriage Gift

A man or woman requested by law or custom to pay a huge amount of marriage gift to his or her partner would feel that an impediment has been placed between him and his lover, that impediment which is immaterial to the meaning of love. The concept of *Mahr* in Islam is neither an actual nor symbolic price for the woman, as was the case in certain cultures, but rather, it is a gift symbolizing love and affection toward the woman of one's dreams. It's specifically decreed that a woman has the full right to her *Mahr*, and that such ownership does not transfer to her father or husband. Sometimes, *Mahr* is used as a shackle to prevent a man from seeking divorce, if fault lines begin to appear on top of the Love Mountain.

If Muslims around the world had executed the payment of *Mahr* as stipulated by God and His Prophet Muhammad (p.bu.h), it would not have become an impediment that always threatens to extinguish the fire of love between lovers. *Mahr*, according to Islam has no price tag. Islam has not therefore set a particular amount of money to be given to a woman by her lover. The reason is that, it should only act as a symbol of love and affection. The *Mahr* to be given therefore increases and decreases according to the wherewithal of the man involved.

At the apex of the proverbial Love Mountain, lovers see the whole world beneath them. They see the forest surrounding them; they also see the rivers flowing beneath; they do also see others hoping to get up to where they are. They see the rainbow of love above them. They breathe in the fresh air of love. They eat love and drink love. *Mahr*, although, an integral part of marriage in Islam should not become a hindrance at this juncture. In order to demonstrate to lovers how *Mahr* should not be a hindrance, the Prophet of Islam, did not demand from his cousin Ali a huge amount of *Mahr* as parents demand today for their daughters (or is it for themselves?). The Prophet only told Ali: "Give her something." Ali then replied: "I have nothing (to give her)." The Prophet then asked him: "Where is your armor?" Ali then answered: "It's with me." The Prophet said: "Then give that to her."[1] Far from thinking that she had been given away cheaply to Ali in marriage; the Prophet's daughter, Fatima, did accept Ali's marriage gift willingly. The Prophet's action was meant as an indicator to the fact that, although *Mahr* is an integral part of Muslim marriage, it must not be an impediment to lovers at the top of the Love Mountain. Ali presented an armor to Fatima because he could not have afforded to give her anything more than that. Had he something more he would not have hesitated to give to his fiancée—the beloved daughter of the Messenger of God.

The Prophet of Islam did witness the marriage of a woman from the Bani Fazaarah tribe that was consummated based on a pair of sandals as the marriage gift. The Prophet asked this woman during the marriage ceremony: "Do you approve of your own accord a pair of sandals as a marriage gift?" She answered "yes," the Prophet then endorsed the marriage."[2] She answered in the affirmative because *Mahr*, or marriage gift became valueless in the eyes of true love that had already settled in their hearts, and had 'crowded out' any potential impediment on their way to marriage. Love is priceless, therefore this woman did not want

1.   Related by *Abu Da'ud, Al-Nasaai* and *Al-Hakim* in their collections of the Prophet's traditions.
2.   Related by *Ahmad, Ibn Majah* and *Al-Tirmidhi* in their collections of the traditions of the Prophet.

'the luster of gold' to inveigle their relationship down the drain. The above narrative also vindicates the high esteem accorded to a woman by Islam. This is the Messenger of God, asking a woman about her opinion concerning something that mattered to her. With this, the rights of a woman were upheld by Islam since fourteen hundred years ago. It's just unfortunate that many Critics might point out that the above episode took place almost a century and a half ago, and that it would no longer hold true in this "Digital Age". Lessons derived from this episode are irrelevant to time and place. Rather, it's the true meaning of love that has been called to attention. Love is timeless and priceless. Despite this, Islam does recognize the importance of having a spiritual peace as well as a material well being. As a result, it places no limitation as to how much *Mahr* a lover should give to his fiancée. We find the following verse in the Holy Qur'an:

> "But if ye decide to take
> One wife in place of another,
> Even if ye had given the latter
> A whole treasure for dower,
> Take not the least bit of it back.
> And how could ye take it when ye
> Have gone in unto each other, and
> They have taken from you a solemn Covenant."[3]

The Arabic word *Qintar* used in this verse translates as a "Talent of Gold". By analogy, it means 'a whole treasure'. It is clear in this verse that, Islam does not prohibit giving a whole treasure as a marriage gift or *Mahr* to a woman, despite the fact that, it is best to follow the teachings and practice of the Prophet of Islam by making it affordable. In a nutshell, although a huge *Mahr* is permissible, it is not recommended. More important than this is true love. In pre-Islamic Arabia, a trick to detract from the freedom of married women was to treat them badly and force them to sue for a *Khul'a*—divorce or it's equivalent in pre-Islamic custom; when, in such a case, a dower could be claimed back. Islam forbade this. This harshness could be exercised in another way—a divorced woman could be prevented by those who have control over her from remarrying; unless she remits her dower. By so doing, the meaning of love that should have been the reason for marriage in the first place is completely lost.

---

3.   Qur'an, 4: 21-22.

In this same verse, the fake lover is rebuked: "And how could ye take it (the dower), when ye have gone in unto each other, and they have taken from you a solemn covenant?" As a woman surrenders her person in marriage, so the man also must surrender at least some of his property according to his means. And in the new relationship created, the parties are recommended to act toward each other with the greatest confidence. "When ye have gone unto each other" implies making love to each other. Here, the man is expected to be a true and trusted lover, and to avoid sexual chicanery. A true lover is not the type who pays a huge sum of money to a woman (as a marriage gift), with a sinister motive of "slipping between the sheets" with her, and later turning around playing tricks in order to get his money back. "…And they have taken from you a solemn covenant." What is this solemn covenant referred to in this verse? It is the marriage contract you have signed with your lover—which entails according her the necessary support, love and rights, as she deserves.

The Prophet of Islam has again placed two important conditions for true lovers at the top of the Love Mountain who plan to get married—religiosity and good moral conduct. An expensive *Mahr* or marriage gift should not impede true lovers who are already on top of the Love Mountain. Religiosity and a good disposition, when present between lovers, would make them live in the nirvana of a perfect marriage. When and if an expensive marriage gift is imposed upon a man who aspires to marry his lover, and even if he manages to pay this amount, he might from time to time look at his lover scornfully as if she had kidnapped him. As if she had actually been bought with money—not with love. As soon as the man begins to think this way about his lover, his love for her begins to wane until such a time that, a small misunderstanding between them leads to a "whole roomful of horrors" like burning his lover's face with acid, or even killing her. The less severe of these horrors might just be a divorce. The reason would have been that, the expensive marriage gift imposed upon him did effectively replace his true love for his partner. Some acts of lovers toward each other are explainable only through an examination of the concomitant circumstances.

It's therefore, unfortunate that, despite the above reasons for not imposing expensive marriage gifts on men, some individual families in the Middle East are still adamant. If all families imposed affordable marriage gifts, there would not have been hatred, insults and even divorce in our homes. The true meaning of love has been lost among those Muslims who remain adamant with regards to the imposition of expensive marriage gifts. All controversies regarding the marriage gift would have been avoided, if all Muslims adhered to the clear teachings of the Messenger of God, Muhammad (p.b.u.h). Have they forgotten what the Prophet of Mercy and Affection had said? "Surely the marriage with the greatest blessing is that (marriage) whose provisions are less burdensome."[4] And in another occasion the Prophet said: "The best women of my *Ummah* (community) are those whose marriage gifts are the least expensive, and those with the most graceful countenances." By aiming to make love the bedrock of every marriage, Islam has made marriages less burdensome on lovers. The aim of Islam is to ensure that the feeling of affection and tenderness between lovers is not compromised due to expensive marriage gifts.

There are often times when a woman would think that asking her man to pay only a pittance as her marriage gift would belittle her in the eyes of her peers or make her look cheap. They might be right in some cases. How sweet to recall the halcyon days of youth! As a youth growing up in Ghana, there was a time, I noticed two married women 'barking' at each other like dogs. And, although it was anathema for children to be found loitering around where grown-ups were quarreling, I managed to stick around as other kids were being chased away with canes! These women were the first and second wives of one man. And, although, I was unaware of the reason behind this fracas, what I heard was interesting. "You are a nonentity, how much did "Alhaji"[5] pay for your dower, was it not only two fowls?" The other woman retorted bitterly: "What of you, you think I don't know what Alhaji gave out as your dower, wasn't it just two bags of millet?" They were arguing furiously. All this while, Alhaji had been out of town—being unaware his house was on fire! I was then too young to understand all these. I became disinterested and left.

First of all, monogamy, to say the least, is alien to African culture. Therefore, it is not surprising to see an Alhaji having as many as four wives. Secondly these two rivals were revealing each other's secrets in the eyes of strangers which was unbecoming of them. Arguing over the amount of dower paid to each woman was irrelevant. What is relevant here is love! These two women had forgotten that they were already on top of the Mountain of Love—that they had already been 'bought' by Alhaji with his love—not with bags of millet and fowls. Of course

---

4.   Sabiq, *Fiqh Al-Sunnah,* 138.
5.   In Sub-Saharan Africa, an Alhaji is someone who has been to Mecca on pilgrimage. A person might even 'hate' you if you, despite your knowledge of he or she being an Alhaji or Hajia (for women), you still fail to address him or her by that title. *Al-Hajj* is an Arabic word denoting pilgrimage: The Pilgrimage to Mecca, or simply the Pilgrim. The real names of some Alhajis and Hajias have been lost or are unknown due to the frequent use of these "titles". For instance, Where is Alhaji or Hajia? Or I'm looking for Alhaji or Hajia. Given names are often lost!

other unmarried women hearing what had transpired between these two rivals would try to avoid falling into the same pit. Finally, the casualty is going to be true love. It is small wonder that the true meaning of love has been lost in our present world. Why do we feel shy about being in love? Why do we feel shy to admit that we had been 'bought' with love and not with money? The above episode compares favorably with one female university graduate in Nigeria, "Ngozi" who would not marry her lover unless he gives out four cows as a dower. The argument was that, as a graduate, she deserved better. She was right.

"I will never marry that man; "Alhaji Danjuma", if he fails to at least give out four cows as a marriage gift to me...after all, he's an illiterate". Ngozi asserted with confidence. "Then why do you even think of marrying him, knowing very well that he's an illiterate; or is it because he's famously rich?" An advocate of true love questioned Ngozi. "No," Ngozi denied. "But what has four cows got to do with your love for Alhaji who is rich but illiterate?" The questioner insisted. An eerie silence ensued. The questioner continued: "Choose one: Four cows or true love from Alhaji (Danjuma often dropped for convenience); because, you can't eat your cake and have it." "But are you sure I will get true love from Alhaji Hm...these Alhajis...my asking Alhaji to pay four cows as a dower is customary; it's not me who is demanding them for my self; it's meant for the 'elders' and for our customary rites, not for me Ngozi!" She insisted. The questioner began to look pensive when he heard what she had said about elders and customary rites. Ngozi continued: "I swear if Alhaji fails to pay four cows as a dower, all my love for him will disappear...he must give out those four cows or else..."

At this point, the questioner became so shocked that he ended the conversation. What should true lovers do if there happens to be a clash between customs and love? The question now is, Why did Ngozi choose to marry this man, despite the fact that they were incompatible intellectually, physically and socially? This was a young trendy and beautiful graduate vis-a-vis an old; bald-headed; old-fashioned; big belly and illiterate man? Was it because Alhaji was famously rich? Or was it because Ngozi thought she could have financial security by getting married to this man, while at the same time holding fast to her boyfriend? Or was she likely to succeed in killing two birds with one stone? Did she bother about having a secure and loving relationship with this man? Was she afraid that her friends would ridicule her if she accepted something less for her dower? But what had been wrong with this Alhaji too? Why was he so recalcitrant in "doling out" four cows as a marriage gift to his "sweetheart" Ngozi? He was so rich that he could even have afforded to buy a BMW for her? At least, it could make her feel proud and "loved". Was Alhaji reserving the gift of a BMW to Ngozi for a rainy day; or was he only being mean? Alhaji knew he could not have avoided offering Ngozi a marriage gift, however, the idea of "four cows" bothered him so much. In this case, Who is the true lover? It's left to the reader to decide. However, what this writer knows all too well is that; each time the forces of true love have reached out to engulf lovers; the forces of fake love have lashed out at them!

How big should the 'Wedding Cake' be?

When two lovers get to the apex of the Love Mountain, they face two issues—at least from the Islamic point of view—the payment of dower or marriage gift, and the holding of the marriage ceremony. From an Islamic point of view, a wedding is expected to take place not long after the dower has been paid. It could, however, be delayed due to a force majeure. Another issue of importance is, How do we compare love with the nature of a wedding ceremony? In other words, How do we know how much two partners love each other by observing the size of their wedding breakfast or wedding cake? Does a small wedding breakfast or cake signify no love or little love? Does a big wedding breakfast or cake signify great love? Before answering this question, this writer believes that common sense tells us of a gap between the knowledge that comes from books and the wisdom that comes from virtue. There may be times when we can weigh and measure knowledge, but I'm convinced that, we can never weigh and measure wisdom. In short, wisdom is not only derived on top of the graduate school mountain. It can also be found on a sandbox at nursery school.

If we agree that wisdom means good judgement; common sense; wise thoughts; or simply the quality of being wise, there is existing evidence in the Holy Qur'an indicating that wisdom could also be obtained during youth:

> "O Yahya! Take hold of the
> Book with might: And we gave
> Him wisdom even as a youth."[6]

The instruction to Yahya (John the Baptist) was clear: "Keep fast hold to God's revelation with all your might: for an unbelieving world has either corrupted it or neglected it. John the Baptist was to prepare the way for Jesus, who was coming to renew and re-interpret it. The Arabic word. *Hukm* translated Wisdom implies something more than Wisdom; it is the wisdom of judgement that is

---

6.   Qur'an, 19:12.

entitled to judge and command, as in the matter of denouncing sin. Then in terms of true love what do we say of lovers who are so ostentatious that they invite scorn and armed robbers upon themselves? Is it part of wisdom to dine and wine so much during their wedding that couples go home with minds befuddled by too much drinking that they even find it difficult to locate their marital bed? What is the glory in this?

Let's be honest, holding a wedding ceremony for two lovers does not occur until the 'bell of love' has rung several times inside the hearts of these two lovers who are already at the top of the Love Mountain—reminding them that, something needs to be done urgently. There is therefore a need to answer to this urgent call. Answering to this call entails the announcement of a wedding ceremony that indicates a desire to live together forever after. The Prophet of Guidance and Mercy, Muhammad (p.b.u.h) said: "Do make an announcement of this wedding ceremony, and let this announcement be in the mosque, and do beat the drums to acknowledge it."[7] By analogy, the announcement of a wedding could be done through microphones in the mosques or through the media or according local customs—provided the way it is done does not contravene the teachings of Islam. In order to venerate the love between these two couples, Islam recommends another form of proof—sacrificing an animal—so that both the rich and the poor would partake of it's simple meal. So that they the attendees of this simple ceremony would invoke the blessings of God upon this couple and wish them a very long and enduring love throughout their being together.

The prophet did ask one of his companions, Abdul-Rahman the son of Auf, to make a wedding party by saying: "Make a wedding party, if even it is with a sheep," he also said: "The worst type of meal is that of a wedding party to which the rich are invited, and the poor are kept out."[8] The reason is that it is rather the poor who are really in need of this meal than the rich. And their invitation is an act of getting closer to God. This is the manner in which the Islamic wedding should be consummated—the announcement of the wedding, the sacrifice of an animal and finally the invitation of people, both the rich and the poor. How many Royal and Star-studded weddings, that are often pomp-laden have foundered after only a few years? It is also true that some Muslims are heedless of the teachings of their religion regarding hosting weddings. In several Muslim communities in the Middle East, Asia and Africa, there has always been a tendency to

---

7. Related by *Ahmad* and *Al-Tirmidhi* in their collections of the traditions of the Prophet.
8. Related by *Al-Bukhari* in his authentic collections of the traditions of the Prophet.

mutual and powerful urge to meet each other (after the wedding) has only been an expression of the true love they have had for each other long before this time. It is love that had been built upon a very solid foundation—God-consciousness, which derives it's roots from the teachings of Islam. Truly, these are two souls that are now being cleansed by the spring water of love that gushes forth from the Love Mountain as they stand on it's top. Presently, there exists a wide gap between what Islam has brought to us, and what we witness in parts of today's Middle East (including some Muslim communities in both Africa and Asia). It is therefore left upon true lovers wishing to prolong their love to uphold the teachings of Islam that does not over-burden them just because they have fallen in love. God tells us in the Holy Qur'an

> "…Allah intends every facility for you,
> He does not want to put you to difficulties…"
> "…No soul shall have a burden laid on it
> Greater than it can bear…"[10]

Unfortunately, the trend is now toward the materialistic and the acquisitive; indeed, there are so many goodies out there to be acquired; and people want more of everything. Consequently, the virtue of true love is now wearing thin.

The Need to replace Sex Education with Love Education

The guiding principle in all relationships should be true love. The hydra-headed problem is always how to winnow cheese from chalk. It is not this writer's intention to criticize any relationship, whether real or imagined, but to make a trenchant observation of the sorry state of romantic relationships in this increasingly materialistic world. The future is bleak for true love. It may happen that, 50 years from now, it will become so endangered that, it might need protection from the United Nations. The establishment of a new sister organization of the United Nations is therefore imperative. It could be named The United Nations High Commission for True Love (UNHC-TL).

In order to realize the objective of setting up the UNHC-TL, The United Nations could have, as a first step, set up a Committee of Eminent True Lovers (CETL); that could include, but not limited to the following international per-

---

10. Qur'an, 2:185, 233.

sonalities: Kofi Annan, the UN Secretary-General, bearing in mind that he is a true lover. Former US Vice President, Al Gore, could also be a member. Former US President, Bill Clinton, is a true lover in his own right; but I have reservations of him joining the list, due to the Lewinsky scandal. I do also have similar reservations about Charles, the Prince of Wales. "I once heard him on the telephone in his bath…and he said, 'Whatever happens, I'll always love you,'" The late Diana, the People's Princess said. "And I told him I'd listened at the door…we had a filthy row."[11] Diana was complaining about Charles' continued relationship with Camilla Parker Bowles after her marriage to him. Former and current British Prime Ministers; Margaret Thatcher and Tony Blair could also have made it into the list; despite the fact that this writer opposes the latter's reasons for going to war with Iraq—weapons of mass destruction are yet to be uncovered. Blair is however a great family man. I admire him for this. Former *Perestroika* and *Glasnost* chief, Mikhail Gorbachev of the former Soviet Union; is also a respected true lover.

Other prominent international figures that could be included in this Committee of Eminent True Lovers would have been current US Secretary of State, Colin Powell; In Africa, Libyan leader Colonel Muammar Qadhafi; former President of Ghana, Jerry John Rawlings, could have been some of these. Although, he too, could be a true lover in his own right; Nelson Mandela, former South African President could have problems joining the list—despite his international standing. Mandela was arrested just six years after he wed Madikizela-Mandela, who gained heroine status during her subsequent years of detention, banishment and arrest. However, when he was freed in 1990, he divorced Winnie Madikizela-Mandela in 1996 for adultery; but she remains popular with poor black South Africans, who still regard her as the former "Mother of the Nation". In the Middle East, The Palestinian Authority President, Yasser Arafat would have been a member.

In Asia former Malaysian Prime Minister, Dr. Mahathir Muhammed; former Chinese President Jiang Zemin; the reclusive North Korean strongman, Kim Jong-il, would not also have been left out. The President of the Philippines, Gloria Macapagal Arroyo, could also have been part of this list. This should have been the case despite her pre-occupation with battling Muslim separatists in the south of her country. The last but not the least would have been current President of Taiwan, Chen Shui-Bian; who has been a true lover to his wheel-chair bound wife, Wu Shu-Chen, since she was injured in an accident almost twenty

---

11.   *MSNBC, In Tapes, Diana speaks of marriage woes, 2.*

years ago. Wu has been paralyzed from the waist down after she was run over by a truck in 1985. An incident believed to be a political attack, as her husband, the President, was then a leading opposition leader in the days of martial law in Taiwan.[12] Hollywood stars like Arnold Schwarzenegger—current California Governor; and Mel Gibson, are all true lovers in my mind. They would have helped educate the world about true love; and also helped in replacing Sex Education with Love Education.

---

12.   *China Post* (Taipei), 16 September 2004.

6

THE DIPLOMACY OF LOVE

The classical definition of diplomacy is "the application of intelligence and tact to the conduct of official relations between the governments of independent states."[1] In the author's view, the *diplomacy of love* involves the "the active use of the mind (not the heart), in the conduct of any romantic relationship between two lovers that borders on the concept of who gets *what*, *when* and *how* in that relationship". According to Harold Nicholson, seven qualities are indispensable for successful diplomats: truthfulness, precision, calmness, good temper, patience, modesty and loyalty. Truthfulness is essential because it contributes to a good reputation, which enhances a diplomat's long-range credibility and subsequent effectiveness. Precision is what Nicholson calls intellectual and moral accuracy. Intellectual accuracy is the faithful description of the reality perceived by the diplomat.

Moral accuracy is the ability of the diplomats to express their views and interpretations boldly and to avoid providing the home office equivocal, ambiguous or politically compatible reports. Calmness, good temper and patience permit diplomats to maintain the detachment and precision of true professionals. Modesty is a central quality: All good diplomats should studiously avoid vanity and should not be flattered, or, worse, boast about their diplomatic victories and successes. In fact they should try to play down even genuine successes and let them appear as fair compromises. Finally, diplomats must be loyal to their governments, their ministries, their own staffs, their fellow diplomats, and to a certain degree, the host country. Their highest loyalty, naturally, should be reserved for their country's overall foreign-policy objectives. For any romantic relationship to be successful all the above-mentioned qualities are needed in one or both—preferably

---

1. Theodore A. Couloumbis and James A. Wolfe, *Introduction to International Relations: Power and Justice* (Englewood Cliffs: Prentice, 1982), 135-136, quoting Harold Nicolson, "The 'Old and New Diplomacy'," in *Politics and the International system*, 2nd ed., ed. Robert L.Pfaltzgraff (Philadelphia: Lippincot, 1972), 425.

both of the partners involved. After all, who would not like to see all of these qualities in his or her partner who claims to be a true a lover? It should, however, be noted that, in the *diplomacy of love*, we are not talking about governments and their foreign–policy objectives, rather what we are concerned here is about the conduct of a romantic relationship between two "consenting individuals".

The Rules of the Game

As a newly wed, memories of a sweet and simple wedding have passed. But has it carried along with it that love which had existed between them long before this wedding? Has the throbbing pulse of love, tenderness, affection and mercy vanished after the wedding night? The answer is to be found in the Holy Qur'an:

> "And among His signs
> Is this, which He created
> For you mates from among
> Yourselves, that ye may
> Dwell in tranquility with them,
> And He has put love and Mercy
> Between your (hearts): Verily
> In those are signs for those who reflect."[2]

It is that type of love that is based upon kindness and friendliness. It has indeed settled in the innermost core of the heart that in turn generates a longing for each other. It is that type of true love which has fallen upon the soul, the senses and the entire body. In this manner, lovers find in each other, a peace of mind, reassurance and a deep-rooted sense of security. The love between them continues to grow every other day—defying time and place. It indeed compares favorably with a waterfall whose water increases rather than decreases—all because this is a type of love that has been based upon the purity of purpose—not upon deception by sophistry. In order to deepen the love between them, the woman's right is emphasized by the Qur'an, and strongly recommended by the Prophet of Islam. The Qur'an states:

---

2.   Qur'an, 23: 21.

"...Live with them on a footing
of kindness and equity, for if ye
hate them, it may happen that
Ye hate a thing and God brings
About through it, a great deal of good."[3]

The Prophet Muhammad (p.b.u.h) said: "The best of you is the best to his family, and I am the best among you to my family. The most perfect believers are the best in conduct, and the best of you are those who are best to their wives."[4] Who is the "best man to his family"? Is he the one whose wedding cake is the biggest; the one who buys the most expensive wedding ring for his fiancée; the one who provides for all the needs of the family in terms of food, money and clothing? Nay! There is something, if not present, renders all the above meaningless. It is indeed love! It is indeed compassion and tenderness, affection and empathy. Is the best of you to your family the one who plays night baseball or watches TV deep into the night leaving his partner groaning, moaning and craving for sex? The Prophet of Islam did had a good deal of prescience about what was likely to happen between two married couples when he reminded lovers that: "No believing man should loathe a believing woman, should it happens that he hates a particular trait in her, it's likely he might love something good about her too."[5] Accordingly, any person intending to destroy the loving relationship between a married couple is considered to be outside the pale of Islam. Indeed, he or she has no honor in claiming any affiliation to it. The Prophet said: "Any one who spreads scandal about a woman to her husband is not part of us."[6]

The door leading to hatred that is likely to occur in a loving relationship has therefore, been slammed in the face of those fake lovers who wish to pass through it. After all, in every loving relationship, there has always been a thin line between love and hate. The prevailing ambience should be nothing but mutual affection and magnanimity. Should it happen that there appears any disturbance in their relationship, they should endeavor to expel it. The act of expelling disturbances is workable only if they cast their memories back in time to the covenant that has existed between them—and which they now seem to be forgetting—the covenant of affection and love, the covenant of companionship and compassion. The

---

3.   Qur'an, 4:19.
4.   Related by *Ibn Hanbal* in his collections of the Prophet's traditions.
5.   Sabiq, *Fiqh Al-Sunnah*, 161.
6.   Related by *Abu Da'ud* and *Al-Nassa-i* in their collections of the Prophetic traditions.

unfettered love between them should not be allowed to deteriorate into nit-picking picayune disputes. In a letter written in 1792, Thomas Jefferson (1743-1826), the third President of the United States of America wrote: "Let what will be said or done, preserve your sang-froid immovably, and to every obstacle, oppose patience, perseverance and a soothing language."[7] Although this was not a letter written by Jefferson to all true lovers, this writer believes all lovers should pay heed to this beautiful advice. I regard this as an essential ingredient in the *diplomacy of love.*

And, although Jefferson might have known very little about the Holy Qur'an, the advice of this great man speaks volumes for lovers, and indeed, it is in conformity with a similar advice given to believing men and women in the Holy Qur'an:

> "Ye shall certainly be tried and tested
> In your possessions and in yourselves;
> And ye shall certainly hear much that
> Will grieve you…but if ye persevere
> Patiently, and guard against evil,—then
> That indeed is matter of great resolution."[8]

The Arabic word *Sabr* implies many shades of meaning, which is impossible to comprehend in one English word. It implies (1) patience in the sense of being thorough, not hasty; (2) patient perseverance, constancy, steadfastness, firmness of purpose; (3) systematic as opposed to spasmodic or chance action; (4) a cheerful attitude of resignation and understanding in sorrow, defeat or suffering, as opposed to murmuring or rebellion; but saved from mere passivity or listlessness. All these qualities, when inherent in any romantic relationship, would save it from going down the drain. Add to this our battles against the vicissitudes of life—not wealth and possession (or the want of them), are the means of our trial. All our personal relationships, the color of our skin, talents, knowledge, opportunities and their opposites; in fact everything that happens to us and makes up our personalities is a means of our testing. So is our faith in God; and in our love for a particular woman or man from a different racial or cultural background. For instance, a Taiwanese lady being married to a dark-skinned man from *Fei-chow*

---

7.   Norman Schur, *1000 Most Important Words*, (New York: Ballantine Books, 1982), 203.

8.   Qur'an, 3:186.

(Africa in Chinese); or a white lady married to a dark or yellow-skinned man any-where in the world. We will have to put up (for our love), many insults from those who do not share with us the "universality of romantic love". Lest I forget! Or a beautiful Arab girl being in love with a dark-skinned African man!

If lovers are unable to address each other with a soothing language; and cannot oppose obstacles between them with patience; mutual hatred develops. Which in turn leads to lovers distancing themselves from each another. The man then finds excuses to be unfaithful, there and then, the love that existed between them turns into a breeze that wafts it's way through the window and out of the marital home—as if it had never existed. This is exactly what is happening in this our "Digital Age". It's happening because the meaning of love has not been well digested by some of us. We are now marrying later than our parents and divorc-ing faster. There are men in this "Age" who still beat their wives. The Prophet of Mercy and Guidance, Muhammad (p.b.u.h), wondered more than fourteen hun-dred years ago, why a man would beat his wife and said: "Any one of you would willfully flog his wife, like the flogging of a slave, and then perhaps would have sexual intercourse with her later the same day."[9] How would a man beat up his wife in the morning, and then later have sex with her in the evening? Can love and hate become bedfellows?

In the *diplomacy of love*, the nature and quality of interactions between lovers indicate the intensity of the existing love between them. Consider for a moment, what Diana, the People's Princess had to say about the quality of her interactions with Charles—The Prince of Wales: "I threw my self down the stairs bearing in mind I was carrying a child," she said, describing *one incident* (emphasis added). "Queen (Elizabeth) comes out, absolutely horrified, shaking she's so fright-ened...*and Charles went out riding*"[10] (emphasis mine). The Princess died at age 36 in a 1997 auto accident in Paris with her companion, Dodi Al Fayed. We are all prisoners of love. Sometimes we are held hostage to loveless relationships to which we have not contributed. At different stages in our lives, we all have to face the real world of romance—that could be unfair and unkind. As the Chinese say-ing goes: "It is very easy to summon up a ghost, but not nearly as easy getting rid of it." In my own words, it is very easy to fall in love, but not nearly as easy falling out of love. Falling in love these days is the hardest thing to do. You really cannot tell who would be the best *diplomat* in a romantic affair. It is equally harder to stay aloof from romance, unless, of course, one has vowed to remain celibate.

9.   Qanbas *Al-Hubb Fil- Islam*, 74.
10.   *MSNBC, In Tapes Diana speaks of marriage woes*, 1

At a time that there exists true love between a married couple, there is bound to be a mutual feeling of affection and tenderness toward one another. If a wife's love for her husband were intense, she would definitely not hesitate to play her part in fulfilling her responsibilities toward her husband. These so-called responsibilities are of no practical significance, they are merely acts aimed at proving to the husband how much she loves him. For this reason, the Prophet had said that: "The best of women are those who make their men happy when they look at them; obey them when they instruct them; and when their men are absent, they guard their chastity and their husbands' wealth."[11] Indeed, she is virtuous, loving and caring. She smiles to her husband whenever he looks at her. For this woman, there is no room for frowning or looking at her husband from the extreme ends of her eyeballs. It is all smiles over-flowing with affection and joy. Her love for her man becomes complete when an element of obedience is added to these smiles. If obedience is non-existent, then where is the love?

There is an Arabic couplet that runs: "*Inna al muhibb liman yuhibb mutee-un.*" Which means that; a lover would naturally obey the one being loved. However, there exists a limit as to how far this obedience should go. As I explained elsewhere in Chapter three, God is considered the source of all love in Islam. Therefore, if this act of obedience would lead one to contravene the provisions of the Islamic code, then there will be no need for it. For instance, if a man, motivated solely by pecuniary interests, forces his wife to indulge in prostitution; and she, knowing very well that prostitution is discouraged in Islam; is expected to disobey him. The Prophet said: "Let there be no obedience toward a creature if that (obedience) results in rebellion against the Creator." Here again, we are told by the Prophet that a true lover of a woman guards her chastity when her husband is absent from home. This means that love and betrayal are strange bedfellows. It cannot be love during his presence and betrayal during his absence. A woman who claims to be a true lover would not entertain another man during the absence of her husband. Rather, her mind would only be occupied with the thoughts of her absent husband—leaving no room for her to even contemplate fooling around.

Indeed her heart would be a fortress of love that entertains no one else but her husband. The same could be said of a man too. He is required to reciprocate the love given to him by his wife. There should be a win-win situation in the *diplomacy of love* in any romantic relationship. A loving wife is also supposed to guard the property of her husband and not squander it during his absence from home.

---

11. Sabiq, *Fiqh-Al-Sunnah*, 172.

The man too is required to provide his wife with adequate financial support. After all, money is not love but money supports love. Islam sees a woman, whether individual or married as an individual in her own right. With the right to own and dispose of her property and earnings without any guardianship over her (whether that be her father, husband, or anyone else). She has the right to buy and sell, give gifts and charity, and may spend her money as she pleases. A marriage gift that is given to her before marriage by the groom is for her personal use, and she may also keep her own family name, rather than taking her husband's. Irrespective of all these, the man is still required to fulfill his conjugal duties toward her according to his means.

The rules of the game in a romantic relationship between married couples in Islam are clear and in harmony with upright human nature. In consideration of the physiology and psychological make-up of man and woman, both have equal rights and claims on one another, except for one responsibility—that of leadership. This is a matter which is natural in any collective life and which is consistent with the nature of man. This brings us to the concept of the *diplomacy of love*—the "active use of the mind" to determine who gets *what*, *when*, and *how* in a romantic relationship. The Qur'an states:

> "…And they (women) have rights
> Similar to those (of men) over them,
> According to what is equitable, but men
> Have a degree above them."[12]

Such degree is maintenance and protection. This refers to that natural difference between the sexes, which entitles the weaker sex to protection. It implies no superiority or advantage before the law. Yet man's role of leadership in relation to his family does not mean dictatorship over his wife. Islam tries to maintain the married state as far as possible, especially where children are concerned, at the same time, it is against the restriction of the liberty of men and women in such vitally important matters as love and family life. It will check hasty action as far as possible, and leave the door of reconciliation open at many stages. Even after divorce, a suggestion of reconciliation is made. In order that the existing love between couples is not "trapped in inertia", there is always the need for lovers to develop unique gifts of cutting through complex issues affecting their relationships and forging consensus. But how can lovers really cut through complex

---

12.   Qur'an, 2:28.

issues affecting their relationships if they hesitate to sit on the bargaining table to negotiate between themselves the nitty-gritty of their relationships—who gets *what*, *when* and *how* in that relationship?

It is however imperative that a woman does not desert the marital bed based on flimsy excuses. There are those women who reason speciously that—it is always the man who needs the sex—not her. Indeed, they are ambivalent about sex. They need the sex, but hate to express it in words and deeds. As a result, they move around the marital home with a sense of insensitivity toward sex. "After all, if he needs me, he would come to me…and even if he does, I will make it a bit tough for him." A housewife asserted. We often hear of a man "raping" his wife, how could this happen between true lovers? One's romantic relationship can be wrecked by such gauche manners. The problem here is that, this attitude could force a man to satisfy his sexual cravings through other means.

Sex is not a thing to be ashamed of, or to be treated lightly, or to be indulged to excess. It is as solemn a fact as anything is in life. This author had an acquaintance who occasionally strayed out of the marital bed with the reason being that: "Anytime I needed sex, my wife always found excuses to deny it to me…so it is not my fault…" Where is the *diplomacy of love* in this marital home? Who gets *what*, *when* and *how* in this relationship? The following verse in the Qur'an calls lovers to attention on matters regarding sex:

"Your wives are as a tilth
Unto you, so approach
Your tilth when and how
Ye will…"[13]

Notice the words, *when* and *how*—denoting the Arabic word, *Haithu*–a comprehensive word referring to manner, time or place. The most delicate matters are here referred to in the most discreet and yet helpful terms. In sex, morality, manner, time and place are all important. Anal sex does not fall into the *when* and *how* category in this verse. Islam does not consider it as a decent sexual behavior. The Messenger of God, Muhammad, (p.b.u.h) said: "It is one of the rights of the husband that, if he seduces his wife (craving for sex), she should not deny him, even if she is riding on a camel."[14] This means that riding on the top of a camel is not sufficient as a reason to deny sex to the man you say you love. These injunc-

---

13. Qur'an, 2:223.
14. Qanbas, *Al-Hubb Fil-Islam*, 81.

tions about sex are not meant to make the woman a 'sex slave', as some opponents of Islam would think, they are only meant to deepen the romance and "scoop out" the meaning of love for our understanding.

There is the story of a woman who had been a true lover. She exhibited all the ingredients of true love. Indeed, she had a firm grip of the *rules of the game* in her marriage life; she was diplomatic and considerate toward her husband. This was a story narrated by the Messenger of God, Muhammad (p.b.u.h), to his companions. The Prophet said: "I inquired from a certain woman whose husband was a woodcutter about how she treated her husband and she said: 'My husband is a woodsman—he cuts woods, and gathers wood in the mountains; he then descends to sell them. He then uses his earning to buy what we need in our home. I always share with him that sort of hardship he has to go through for the sake of our livelihood. I also do feel (in me) the severity of the thirst he had to endure in the mountains—that almost always scorched my throat too. Due to this, I always prepared for him a good drinking water—so that anytime he comes back, he finds it readily available. Before he comes home, I tidy up the home (keeping every thing in it's rightful place), then I set the table. After all these, I then put on my most beautiful dress—waiting for his return and; as soon as he enters; I would welcome him in such a manner as a bride would do for a bridegroom with whom she was deeply in love. I would do this in a total submission of my self. Then when he needs rest, I would aid him unto it; then when he needs me, I would fall into his arms (allowing him to play with me) in such a manner as a father would play with his little girl…"[15] This poor and hard-working woodcutter of a man had to endure the scorching sun of Arabia up in the mountains, just to be able to fend for his family. His wife did her part in providing him with a relaxed and conducive ambience.

The Contravention of these Rules

When a man got married to a divorcee and informed the Prophet about it, he said: "Had it been that it were a maiden, in order that both of you engage each other in amorous dalliance. He then informed the Prophet that his father had left behind young girls who are in need of a woman caretaker. And a divorcee was most capable in doing that than a maiden who lacks such an experience."[16] That is not to say that the Prophet discouraged his companions from marrying divor-

15. Ibid., 86.
16. Sabiq, *Fiqh Al-Sunnah*, 19.

cees. Of paramount importance to the Prophet was the continuation of love between the couples. "In order that you engage each other in amorous dalliance." How would a man engage a woman his mother's age in amorous dalliance! Flirtations between a man and his wife are an indication of the continuation of love. After all, love is like a flower that needs to be watered constantly. The 'water' for this flower should be flirting with each other. The Prophet described a man who shies way from having fun with his wife as cruel. He said: "There are three actions that borders on cruelty…and one of them is for a man to have sexual intercourse with his wife without first of all kissing her."[17]

It is tyrannical indeed. Is it only enough to have sex with one's wife to the exclusion of any foreplay? And how many Muslims actually engage their wives in amorous dalliance and real foreplay before making love to them? How many of Muslims today would sweep their wives up into their arms, squeeze the breath out of them, and (in an ecstasy of delight) they cry aloud—Honey! A young Muslim girl in Ghana divorced her 'father–husband'[18] complaining that anytime the man wanted to have sex with her, he only recited the expression *Bismill-aah*—a Qur'anic expression meaning "In The Name of Allah", and then 'pounces' upon her without any foreplay. In essence, he was not romantic. Although it is highly recommended that Muslims, before doing any action (including making love to each other) repeat this expression, this man thought saying *Bismillah* alone did the trick! He was dead wrong! And, although, divorce should be avoided at all cost, a Muslim woman has the right to seek divorce from her husband for the lack of sexual satisfaction. That was exactly what this young girl did.

I had a friend in Ghana who intimated to me that he beats up his wife anytime he wanted to make love to her. At that time, he had two wives. When I asked him the reason behind that, he said his second wife was very stubborn! But does this problem exist in Africa alone? What of the Chinese saying that goes as: "If you do not beat up your wife every three days, she will start tearing up the roof tiles"? Meaning that a wife not beaten is a wife out of control. In either case Islam repudiates such an action—wife beating before sex, and wife beating to assert effective control. I must emphasize, however, that wife beating is not indigenous to any particular region or race. A Cambodian man was so infuriated when he came home and found his wife out and no lunch on the table that, he set fire to the

---

17. Qanbas, *Alhubb Fil-Islam*, 74.
18. I use this term to refer to a man whose daughter is older than his wife. For instance, A 56 year-old man married to a 16 year-old girl.

family house and burnt it to the ground, the Cambodian-language *Rasmei Kampuchea* Daily reported.[19] The 37 year-old husband torched the house *to teach his wife a lesson* (emphasis mine). He then turned himself in to the police. The man was then temporarily detained in a local jail where he was assured of regular meals! Only God knows what would have happened if this man had met his wife inside that family house.

Islam abhors all behaviors that border on bestiality, making individuals wolfish in behavior but human in appearance. The two men mentioned above did not behave like people who have in them the feelings of affection and mercy. They are venting their anger on the 'love of their lives'—those hapless creatures who can ill-afford to defend themselves physically against these attacks from their so-called husbands. The men have forgotten entirely about the 'covenant of love and affection' they had promised their loving wives. Worst still, they have also forgotten that they are already on top of the Mountain of Love, Nay! These are women who have hearts throbbing with compassion and affection, and souls yearning for intimacy and true love. In the light of such treatments, they would feel they have lost the love, dignity, and position they commanded inside the hearts of their 'better halves', and, as a consequence, they could become shell-shocked and frightened that they might contemplate suicide. Would these men, callous as they have been, become contrite and pay heed to *the rules of the game* inherent in the *diplomacy of love?*

There is a Chinese saying that goes as follows: "Even the cleverest woman cannot prepare a meal without rice." This might be the case because rice is considered indispensable in every Chinese meal. It could be said that the "rice" in the *diplomacy of love* is good inter-personal relationship between lovers—whether or not they do agree with each other in a lot of issues. There are three virtues inherent in the *diplomacy of love*: Patience in approach to difficulties arising in a romantic relationship; pragmatism in priorities—who gets *what, when* and *how* in a romantic relationship; and steadiness in values—there is always a danger of infidelity getting the last word. For any relationship to endure, there is the need for both partners to be aggressively innovative on how best to "spice up" their relationship. Monotony in any relationship risks running that relationship into the ground; especially if one partner insists on sticking to his or her way of doing "the same old things"—come hell or high water!

If for instance a man asks his wife to turn on the TV, and she replies by saying that: "You did not marry me to come turn on the TV for you, you better do that

---

19.   *China Post*, (Taipei), 30 November 1999.

by yourself." She feels they are both equal, and therefore, they should both respect each other—no one taking advantage of the other. It's absolutely true that both of you are equal, but turning on the TV does not make you look subservient—it gives you the opportunity to express your love to your partner. It does not behoove a man to ask his wife to turn on the TV with a peremptory command similar to that of a military commander instructing his subordinates. Certainly, some women would carry out this "instruction" with slavish compliance; some others might even refuse to turn on the TV! This reminds me of the famous English poet, William Cowper (1731-1800) who wrote:

> "He would not, with a peremptory tone,
> Assert the nose upon his face his own."[20]

Divorce: An Old Solution to Marital Problems

There are many reasons why there is a rising divorce rate even in the Arab and Islamic countries. The first among these is that, some Muslims do not fully comprehend what Islam has stipulated regarding *how* to create good times between married couples, and *how* to keep these good times rolling. What is meant here is not merely having a cerebral knowledge of *what* should be done to keep the love; rather, the willingness to implement what has been taught by Islam. And if even some Muslims have the willingness to implement the Islamic teachings concerning love, another problem is—*how* do they go about implementing it? In the *diplomacy of love*, there is a need for all lovers to implore the "active use of the mind", not the heart. In every romantic relationship, lovers must be ready to apply two different solutions to one problem. This is related to applying our common sense, our social skills, and having the ability to cope with our emotions. Success in a romantic relationship is all about bridging the gap between principles and practice. For example, "beating up one's wife (or girl friend as the case may be), as a principle every three days; in order to prevent her from getting out of control and start tearing up the roof tiles," could be bridged with an "active use of the mind" to find another solution to this problem.

Unlike the animals and plants, Allah (the proper name for God in Arabic), has endowed human beings with a powerful mind that can be used proactively, imaginatively and responsibly. According to Scientists, the mind thinks at a rate of 1000 words per minute. It is therefore clear that Allah wants us to maximize our

---

20.   Schur, *1000 Most Important Words*, 163.

minds to be positive, resourceful, innovative and constructive so that we can help find solutions to some problems in society. We cannot rely on old solutions to solve marital problems. To this writer, DIVORCE is an OLD SOLUTION in resolving problems associated with marriage. We need to boldly delve for new methods to keep marriages intact, more than ever, this means liberating our thinking, daring to rush forward, daring to act, daring to do what no one else has done before this "Digital Age". Obviously at a point in history, one will reach the saturation point and will need to get rid of the old. And as this writer has observed, divorce is an old solution in resolving marital problems. If even divorce is acceptable in the Qur'an can't we find a better solution than just that?

In order that we find other solutions to marital problems other than divorce, God has described the strong bond between a married couple as *Meethaaqun Ghaleedhz* (a solemn covenant)[21] The Prophet of Islam, Muhammad (p.b.u.h) said: "The most abominable among all permissible things is divorce."[22] If divorce is the most abominable permissible thing, why can't we just tie it to a big rock and throw it into the Bermuda Triangle and forget it?

The second reason why divorce is on the rise in the world could be due to a paucity in numbers among jealous lovers—a jealous woman who loves her husband dearly and loathes to see him in a wrong place at the wrong time, and vice-versa. Referring to a common saying in French: *Pas la jalousie, pas l'amour* (if there is no jealousy, then there is no love), one realizes that jealousy is another expression of love. Love and jealousy are indeed two faces of the same coin. We find an example in Islam, when Sa'ad the son of Ubaadah and a companion of the Prophet; addressed a gathering of the Prophet's companions in his presence in the following words: "By God, O the Messenger of God, if there had been any other person (found) with my wife, I would strike him with this my sword—the companions were astonished—then the Prophet Muhammad (p.bu.h.) said: 'Are you astonished at Sa'ad's declaration? By God, I am more of a jealous man than Sa'ad, and God is more of a Jealous Lord than myself and Sa'ad.'"[23]

I must point out quickly that God's jealousy borders on doing things forbidden by Him, and the association of partners (lesser gods) with Him—equating them to Him, and according them that sort of love that should be reserved to Him alone. Islam warns believers against anthropomorphism—the tendency to conceive of God after our own pattern as being in need of sleep, women, love,

---

21.   Qur'an, 4:21.
22.   Related by *Abu Da'ud* and *Al-Hakim* in their collections of the Prophet's traditions.
23.   Sabiq, *Fiqh Al-Sunnah*, 162.

sons or daughters—we are all His creatures. Who are commanded to obey Him. His nature is so sublime, so far beyond our limited conceptions. He is not like any other person or thing that we can imagine. This was how Sa'ad expressed his love for his wife in the form of jealousy that is approved of by God and His Messenger. It is that type of jealousy that supervises and protects love. It's not the type of jealousy that causes suspicion and borders on the speculative and unreliable. The Messenger of God, Muhammad, said: "There is a type of jealousy that is approved by God and that, which angers Him."[24] Common sense would tell us what type of jealousy is desirable and that which is undesirable between lovers. A measure of diplomacy and a balancing act is needed in juggling two balls in the air—love and jealousy. The other problem associated with divorce is that, it's sometimes very hard for a divorcee who actually wants to re-marry to get another husband in some parts of the world. It is even harder for a widow.

When this writer was a student in Damascus, Syria, he had a good Arab friend called "Adnan" with whom he used to work as a part-time student in a certain Syrian Company. During work, we talked about everything under the sun, the Chinese would say *T'an t'ien, shuo di*—from religion, to the taboo subject of Syrian politics—the iron grip of power by then Syrian President, Hafiz–al Asad. In between, we also discussed romantic affairs (another taboo subject that could not be discussed openly. Adnan, almost 25 by then, had never had a date with a woman, and had never traveled outside Syria. One day, during a very hot summer in Damascus, I discussed with him my desire to marry a Syrian Arab girl. He insisted it would not be possible, rather he suggested I marry one widow—a young girl whose husband had died not quite a long time ago. I knew her father very well, he was "Abu Manaf", who was a driver working with our Company. I could not have informed the bereaved Abu Manaf about my desire to marry his widowed daughter so soon. What I could not understand was Adnan's insistence that I marry this girl, he even offered to "do the talking on my behalf" if I were interested but lacked the effrontery to approach Abu Manaf. I was adamant, all along insisting that; my mind had only been focused on a damsel—not a widow.

Adnan made me understand how unlikely it was for me to marry a damsel, and how "evil" it was to be seen talking to an Arab girl in the bus. Coming fresh from Africa, I had yet to re-discover Islam in an Arab social setting. I knew Adnan was right. His remarks were fairly innocuous. I knew very well that he was a Muslim par-excellence. Despite that, I could not digest his advice easily, because they had no "nutritional value". Like Adnan, I was a Muslim all right,

---

24.   Related by *Abu Da'ud, Al-Nassaai* and *Ibn Habban*, in their traditions of the Prophet.

but what then, was the problem? Was it because I was a DSA?[25] No, I don't think so. All this while, I had already developed a great deal of sympathy for this unfortunate girl who had lost her husband not quite a long time ago. I knew quite well that it would not be easy for her to find someone any time soon—indeed she risked spending the rest of her life in "the waiting room of love", and never finding any one at all. Despite the fact that lifestyles are now changing, in such a society it took a God-fearing person to actually marry a widow or a divorcee.[26] Although being a Muslim from Africa, Adnan did respect me for my knowledge about Islam. After having bombarded my Arab friend with series of homilies, he finally backed down. However, in his heart of hearts, he knew it would be better and much easier for me if I had agreed to settle for a young widow—rather than a damsel.

During the whole of this episode, that took weeks and months, Adnan thought he was behaving rationally, I thought otherwise. After a barrage of religious sermons aimed to correct this "irrational" behavior of his, he soon realized he had behaved strangely–and wanted a way out of it. But time had a sneaky way of slipping away. Adnan and my self became so involved in our disagreements that, before we knew it, the tomorrows became yesterdays, another hot summer had arrived—the summer of 1988. As a young man from Africa who sought knowledge like a desert dweller does for water, and gouged for it like a miner does for diamonds; I knew it was time to leave Syria and move toward the Far East. But I knew I could not have traveled out of Syria before Adnan's marriage to his beautiful cousin. After all, I had every right to enjoy the world's beauty and joie de vivre. So many years have passed since my departure from Syria—a country of honest and hardworking people; a country of Islamic religious knowledge; a country of dreams and adventure; and just before I left—a country where I failed to clinch "a romantic deal". There are still, however, three questions still hanging over my lips and begging for answers. (1) Why didn't Adnan offer to marry that widow of a girl? (2) Was he being "rational"? in asking me to marry her? (3) Had I sinned for my refusal to marry her?

---

25. An acronym coined by this writer denoting "A Dark Skinned African." No racial instigation intended.
26. A March 2004 Program aired by the Arab Satellite TV, *Al-Jazeera*, entitled, *Lin-Nisaai Faqat*, a "Women's Only Program" discussed the fate of widows, divorcees, and marriage in general in the Arab World.

7

LOVE IN A CORRUPT PATRIARCHAL WORLD

It is imperative to state that the status which women have acquired during this present era has not come about due to the kindness of men or due to natural progress. It was rather achieved due to a long and arduous struggle over a period of a century and a half. A Roman wife was described by an historian as: "a babe, a minor, a ward, a person incapable of doing or acting anything according to her own individual taste, a person continually under the tutelage and guardianship of her husband[1]

The Struggle for Equality: A Brief History

Kim Campbell, the first female Defense Minister of Canada one said: "There are still tremendous barriers to women running politics; and if they do win, it is very hard to function in such a male-dominated 'old boys' network atmosphere."[2] Twice divorced, Campbell once described the life of a single woman in politics as unspeakably lonely. As a matter of fact, in terms of women, the whole world is developing. There is no "developed world" when women's economic and political status is the measure, and inequality impedes their progress. That was the consensus among the 15, 000 women—including 2000 Americans who attended the historic World Conference on Women held in Nairobi, Kenya, in 1985. Indeed a study in 1993 of the status of women in 99 countries documented that in no country are women the equals of men in health, education, employment, social security or marriage. Only seven countries were rated "very good" in the study. Eighteen were "extremely poor". Interestingly, countries rated extremely poor in

---

1.   E.A. Allen, *History of Civilization,* vol.3 (Cincinnati: General Publishing House, 1889), 444.
2.   *China Post*, (Taipei), 31 March 1993.

women's status were also extremely poor countries. Poverty and inequality went hand in hand.

It will be recalled that in 1848, Elizabeth Caddy Stanton and Lucretia Mott, both American women, decided to hold a women's rights meeting after their return from London where they were denied participation in the World Anti-Slavery Congress. The result was the famous Seneca Falls meeting in 1848 which could be said to be the beginning of an international conference on women. And also in the year 1888, and in Washington D.C., Stanton and Susan B. Anthony hosted the first International Congress on Women. It's goal was to recognize "universal sisterhood", to address the questions confronting womanhood, and deal with equality and justice (Bell and Offen 1983). This congress led to the organization on the International Council on Women, which held it's centennial celebration in Washington D.C. in 1988. These American women were able to champion the women movements around the world by virtue of their exercising of four U.S. freedoms—that citizens of other countries may have been deprived of—freedom of speech, freedom of association, freedom of publication, and freedom of travel.[3]

Women movements around the world have created new international networks to address a variety of specific issues including domestic violence, women's access to education and health services, and non-discrimination in employment. To be sure, the crimes committed against womanhood have had several implications—from psychological to existential. They are indeed crimes of moral turpitude. We all are aware of the bride burning in some parts of India, and the female genital mutilation (FGM), in some parts of Africa and Latin America. And if we cast a glance at "the mirror of history", we will see that about 1450 years ago; the Desert Arabs of Arabia used to bury their female offspring alive in order to get rid of them, since it was anathema to have a female offspring born into a family. Women generally have also been denied access to education in many parts of Africa and Asia—until recently—thanks to the Women's Lib.

In the short interval of human history, encompassed by the period between Seneca Falls and Nairobi, an increasing number of women around the world have been educated; entered paid employment, become voters, been elected to decision-making positions; become healthier, had fewer children and lived longer. However sexual harassment and rape still remain hydra-headed problems defying

---

3.   For further reading on this topic, see Jill K. Conway and Susan C. Bourque, eds, *The Politics of Women's Education: Perspectives from Asia, Africa and Latin America*, Women and Culture (Ann Arbor: University of Michigan Press, 1993).

easy solutions. Some women have also inadvertently contributed to this problem by engaging in TV commercials—sometimes in sexually offensive postures. In a word, thinking people disdain TV commercials that use pretty girls instead of informative data to sell their products. A woman who makes her self a dazzling display by uncovering her beauty and make up for every body to see excites dormant desires.

The Veneration of Woman in Islam

Islam encourages the husband to treat his wife well, as the Prophet Muhammad (p.b.u.h) said: "The best among you are those who are best to their wives."[4] Mothers in Islam are highly honored. Islam recommends treating them in the best way. A man came to the Prophet and said: "O Messenger of God! Who among the people is the most worthy of my companionship?" The Prophet replied: "Your mother. The man said then who? The Prophet said: Then your mother. The man further asked: Then who? The Prophet said: Then your mother. The man asked again: Then who? The Prophet said: Then your father."[5] The food for thought here is that, in the above quotation, the Prophet mentioned "your mother" three times before then saying "your father."

Monica Lewinsky, Linda Tripp, and others like them may have been oppressed pawns, who had no choice but to use their feminine wiles to negotiate their way in this corrupt patriarchal world. When two people fall in love, they tend to have responsibilities toward each other. In this patriarchal world of ours, the burden of proof rests on the man to show real concern to his partner and accord her the necessary companionship that she desires. God says in the Holy Qur'an:

> "Live with them on a footing
> Of kindness and equity…"[6]

This has been addressed to men—not women. Living with your lovers on a footing of kindness and equity results in the strengthening of the bond between lovers. Regardless of the material comfort a man offers his partner, if he is abu-

---

4.   Narrated by *Ibn Majah* and *Al-Tirmizi* in their collections of the Prophet's traditions.
5.   Narrated by *Muslim* and al-*Bukhari* in their authentic collections of the Prophetic traditions.
6.   Qur'an, 4:19.

sive, treating his partner always with scorn, that sort of tranquility and peaceful co-existence that is supposed to have existed between them will be lost. One of the companions of the Prophet of Islam, Mu'aawiyah the son of Haydah, said: "I asked the Messenger of God: 'O the Messenger of God, what is the right of a wife of any one of us upon him?'" The Prophet then said: "You should feed her as you feed yourself; clothe her as you clothe yourself; do not strike her face; do not use a profane language on her; do not desert her—unless within the marital home."[7] Therefore there is no distinction or preferential treatment for a man at the expense of his wife. Rather the prevailing atmosphere should be that of egalitarianism and fairness. Even on the part of sexual intercourse, a woman has the right to the enjoyment of sex (to the fullest) just like her male counterpart. Like the man, she also has sexual cravings that need to be "toned down". As a matter of fact, the Prophet addressed his companions saying: "Should any one of you engage in sexual intercourse with his wife…and after the satisfaction of his desire, he should not rush her until she also is satisfied…"[8] This literally means that when a man achieves orgasm during sex, he should be considerate and also help his partner achieve the same.

After the Prophet mentioned the rights of a woman to feeding and clothing as veneration to her, he added: "Do not strike her face; do not use a profane language on her." Why should you strike the face of your beloved wife, after you had assured her you loved everything about her face? Why should you utter a stream of profanities on her, even though, during the period of courtship; you talked from your heart into hers—with that sweet and smooth voice flowing with honey—and as you talked to her, your eyes had a sleepy look as if you were the victim of a secondary smoke from an opium den? It is part of showing your love to your wife that you are not supposed to desert the matrimonial home when you get angry. Because your deserting the matrimonial home, leaving your wife alone, will only create a big hole through which Satan passes into her heart. She then starts to become suspicious about you; her feelings toward you might also begin to undergo a gradual change. The "marriage rod" that held your marriage together begins to curve—until such a time that it's back becomes as curved as a bow. At this time, no one, not even counseling or the courts would be able to straighten it. The only solution could be a divorce. In order to preserve the love between them, Islam requires a man to remain inside his home even if he has

---

7.   Sabiq, *Fiqh Al-Sunnah*, 161.
8.   Ibid., 164.

been angered by his wife. This is meant to assure her that, despite the fact that he is angry with her, he still loves her.

If you love something dearly, you guard it jealousy. Likewise, if you possess gold and diamonds, you strive to protect them from being stolen. In order to protect love that is expected to last throughout their marriage lives, the Qur'an addresses women in the following words:

> "And say to the believing women
> That they should lower their gaze
> And guard their modesty; that they
> Should not display their beauty
> And ornaments except what (ordinarily)
> Appear thereof; that they should draw
> Veils over their bosoms and not display
> Their beauty except to their husbands..."[9]

A woman is usually content with the love given to her by her husband (or boyfriend as the case may be), then why the gaze at other men? Why the adornments and show of beauty to other men? The rule of modesty applies to men as well as women. A brazen stare by a man at a woman is breach of refined manners. Where sex is concerned, modesty is not only "good form"; it is not only to guard the weaker sex, but also to guard the spiritual good of the stronger sex. The need for modesty is the same for both men and women; but on the account of the differentiation of the sexes in nature; temperaments, and social life; a greater amount of privacy is required for women than men, especially in the matter of dress and the uncovering of the bosom.

Why shouldn't a woman dress more grandiosely at home just for the eyes of her husband—indirectly telling him that she is "in charge" and no one else? And why shouldn't a man do the same for his wife at home? Instead what we see in our cities today are some women exposing their beauties to attract attention, and some men dressing awkwardly to look "cute". A man at home may not take a bath for three or four days consecutively, but if he gets invited to say, a dinner party, he would dress up smartly. A woman with a live-in boy friend or husband might also stay at home without cleaning up for days. However, when it's time to go out with other friends and knowing that it's likely she might meet other men;

---

9.   Qur'an, 24:31.

she might immediately make an appointment with a hair stylist, not only that; and even a beautician! And in Africa, there are these Muslim women who would look more beautiful only when they are attending weddings, funerals and child-naming ceremonies. What of those unfortunate men they leave behind at home? They are being left to wallow in the whirlpool of romance! Were these not the men you vowed to love with all your hearts? When such men realize they are now in deep 'trouble' regarding their marriage life, they might also start making appointments with plastic surgeons—in order to make changes to their physical appearances—trying to add to, take away from, or make a general overhaul of their eyes, noses, ears, lips and teeth, with the sole intention of becoming more "cute".

Some men might also try to see their dentists to replace their incisors (front teeth) that they lost years back, and which they had neglected for a long time! As they become more "cute", things may then start to fall apart—until the center can no longer hold (to borrow Chinua Achebe's words in *Things Fall Apart*). These men begin to live in other women's world, not that of their wives (or girl friends as the case may be). After a while, when these women realize that their husbands now come back late from work, they also become more aggressive by doing "the same old things"—as a means of retaliating. And instead of trying to reverse such attitudes, they might seek help from soothsayers. In the case of Africa and in some parts of the Arab world some women might employ the services of *le marabout*—a French word used in African parlance denoting a specialist who uses verses of the Qur'an in preparing certain concoctions as a cure to certain types of ailments. They are also fond of preparing love potions for both men and women. Some of these *marabouts* also claim to be able to divine the future. Although some of these are helpful, a majority is unhelpful; they are mountebanks. In *Hamlet* (act IV, scene 7), Laertes tells King Claudius: "I bought an unction of a mountebank."

Winning a man or a woman's love by employing the services of a soothsayer, and for that matter, a *marabout* is a disservice to true love. It doesn't usually stand the test of time. Some believe that good marriages are made in heaven, but this writer is of the opinion that the "maintenance work" must be done right down here by lovers themselves. In a male-dominated world of sex, it's always the woman who finally ends up at the short end of the stick! Others might disagree.

In an attempt to protect the woman from not only being used as a sex object, but from sexual harassment. The Holy Qur'an commands the Prophet Muhammad (p.b.u.h) in the following words:

"O Prohet! Tell thy wives and daughters
And the believing women that they should
Cast their outer garments over their persons
(When out of doors): That is most convenient,
That they should be known (as such) and not
Molested. And Allah is most forgiving,
Most Merciful."[10]

This is for all Muslim women, those of the Prophet's household, as well as the others. They were asked to cover themselves with outer garments when walking out of the door. The object was not to restrict the liberty of women—as Islam's critics say, but to protect them from harm and molestation, and by analogy—sexual harassment. In the East and in the West, a distinctive public dress of some sort or another has always been a badge of honor or distinction, both among men and women. This can be traced back to the earliest civilization. The Assyrian Law in it's palmiest days (say, 7th century B.C.), enjoined the veiling of married women and forbade the veiling of slaves and women of ill fame.[11]

Furthermore, the reason behind the revelation of this verse as explained by Imam Al-Qortobi was that: "Before the widespread use of indoor toilets, women used to relieve themselves in the desert. This would cancel the distinction between free women and women slaves. So Muslim women used to be harassed by the wicked infidels, who thought that they were slaves. When approached by such a man, the Muslim woman used to shout to make him keep his distance. When the women complained to the Prophet (p.b.u.h.), the above verse was revealed [That was when Muslim women started to cover their modesty]. From then onward, the free Muslim women were clearly distinguished from the women slaves."[12]

It seems to this writer that the meaning of true love may soon be buried, (if not) forever in this corrupt patriarchal world. In our corrupt system, love can be described figuratively as "a female infant that has been buried alive". The Holy Qur'an says:

---

10. Qur'an, 33:59.
11. *Cambridge History,* vol. 3, 107.
12. Abdul Hamid Al-Balali, *Mal-Maani' Minal Hajaab?* (Why not Cover your Modesty), trans. Wael F. Tabba' (Dammam: Dar Al-Thakair, 1995), 12, quoting Imam Al-Qortobi, "Tafseer Al-Qortobi," (8/5325).

> "When the female (infant),
> Buried alive, is questioned
> For what crime it was killed."[13]

In this world of sin and sorrow, much unjust suffering is caused, and innocent lives—mostly women and children sacrificed in the name of "love". How many innocent women have been infected with AIDS, without a trace being left, by which "love offenders" can be brought to justice? A striking example during the pre-Islamic period was female infanticide. The crime was committed in the guise of social plausibility in secret collusion, and no question was ever asked. The pagan Arabs believed having a girl child brought a disgrace to the family, so when any of them had a girl-child, they got rid of it by burying it alive—a cruel and an indefensible crime. But in the world of Justice—the day of judgement, full questions will be asked, and the victim herself—unable to speak in this world, will be able to give evidence, for she had committed no crime her self. A fair-minded Orientalist, Professor of Eastern Languages at the University of Geneva, Mr. Edouard Montet, speaking on this subject in his introduction to the translation of the Qur'an writes: "Progress of infinite significance has been realized through these reforms, so that Muhammad can be considered as one of the greatest bene-factors of mankind. Were it only for the absolute interdiction to kill girls at birth, Muhammad would have left an unforgettable memory in the history of his time."[14]

The same could be said about love, it has been used as a means to an end. Love itself is the victim today, it has committed no crime; rather it is people who have used it's good name to indulge in all types of sexual crimes. It is because it has not been love that has caused so much pain and regret to some women and men; rather it has been due to the misuse of the word "love". In this regard, love has been oppressed and may soon be "buried alive" like the female infant in pre-Islamic Arabia! There are daily reports of men defiling children as young as 5 years old in some parts of the globe.

There are those married men who leave their homes during the darkness of the night in order to spend time with their mistresses—leaving their wives deprived of love and affection! These men sometimes return to their homes just before

---

13. Qur'an, 81:8-9.
14. Qouted in "Conferences On Muslim Doctrine And Human Rights in Islam: Between Saudi Canonists and Eminent European Jurists And Intellectuals, Second Conference of Paris, 2 November 1974 (Ministry of Justice: Riyadh and Dar Al Kitaab Allubnani: Beirut, n.d), 170.

daybreak, intoxicated, and with befuddled minds mistake their live-in maids for their wives! There are also those women who betray their husbands, spending several "dark nights" during their absence from home entertaining other men. There has been so much acting about love by our movie stars, and equally too many love songs by well-meaning artists, but has all these been translated into true and enduring relationships? Interestingly, some of these artists who have starred in romantic movies, and others who have sang beautiful songs about love, have not been role models in real life. In this writer's view the increasing number of brothels and "commercial sex workers" all around the world are all by-products of a corrupt patriarchal world. The reasons are more social than they are economic. Those women who desire to marry and raise a family aren't getting true lovers, who would take a better care of their emotional and financial needs. A true lover can be a better "gate-keeper" of the matrimonial home. His love for his partner makes him a better earner, he would detest to see his "First Lady" wallow in poverty or left to rot away in disgrace. The offspring in such a matrimonial home, usually grow up to become useful members of the society and responsible citizens of the world.

Dreams and Deception

"I believed him, an innocent girl lamented, when he said to me: 'I could not have found a better lover had I searched the world for years.'" "Now just look at me, I'm pregnant, and has tested positive to the HIV virus that causes AIDS...it is likely my child would be infected too...the worst thing is that, I have now been abandoned." Unable to hold back tears that flowed freely down her cheeks, she continued: "When I insisted on using a condom, he assured me that I was his first love, and that he would never harm me because he loved me...I thought I would impress him and make him marry me by sleeping with him." In this poignant spectacle, this writer identified two victims—that miserable girl and "love". Love had been misused. Another twenty-something year-old girl pleaded with her boy friend in these words. "If you really love me, why are you insisting that we have sex before marriage?" "After we've had sex, you will understand." Her boyfriend replied. "The reason why I'm insisting we have sex before marriage is precisely because I love you." He retorted bitterly. In the case of the former, who is now HIV positive, her boy friend had planted a seed of hope inside her tender heart—by assuring her she was her first love, but before it took roots, weeds already flourished! She has now been left twisting in the wind! In the latter case, the girl, was luckier, she had resisted all of her boy friend's unnecessary sexual advances to the end.

As I sat on a chair studying Shakespeare one evening in Ghana, 1 came across Polonius' advice to his son Laertes, "Neither a borrower nor a lender be." And as I sat cogitating about it's meaning, one of my distant cousins who was several years older than me, (and had been recently divorced), entered my room. With a wry smile, she said: "Why is it that you men, whenever you need sex, you tend to behave as a dog does when broth is poured upon it's back; and after you achieve orgasm, you tend to forget of your partner...?" One can imagine what a hungry dog does when a bone or chicken broth is put on it's back. For a moment, I neglected her and rather concentrated on what I had been doing. I was then naïve about sex—and still lacked a firm grip on *the rules of the game,* (see the previous chapter), moreover, I saw her interference as a distraction. As she sat quietly looking at the rose flowers on top of the piano in the living room, she murmured: "These rose flowers are as old and tired as the piano it's self." I then sensed that she was about to change the topic, I became interested, putting away my book, I then asked her to repeat what she had said previously.

Despite my pleas, she refused to repeat her earlier statement. To my chagrin, she left the room and slammed the door behind her. After this, the "cognitive wiring" in my brains began to transmit a rather high "voltage" that transformed my entire evening. And, instead of reconsidering Polonius' advice to his son Laertes, I rather found my self in a pensive mood—trying to figure out what my beautiful cousin had said. After all, this had been a young and pretty woman who had been married to a *marabout* (sometimes known as a "Malami" in West Africa), who was several years older than her. Indeed, they never shared anything in common. Had it been that she had been 'persuaded' to marry this man, as is usually the case in some Muslim societies in Africa? Or, was it that she had been divorced (or did she divorce her husband?) due to the fact that her sex life was abysmal? She never did tell me anything; and, being in my late teens I was considered too young (by African standards); in trying to know "whether snakes do have ears"[15]. I was in a dilemma; I could not have asked her about her marriage, but in my young mind, I suspected "sex" was to blame. I did however know that, my cousin's husband—that *marabout*—was as boring and unromantic as a Church mouse!

---

15.   This expression, taken from one African tribe; the Dagomba tribe in Ghana, describes a state of being 'too inquisitive'.

To me, the best way to probe the reason for her unsuccessful marriage was to draw a line out of the past (when she 'agreed' to marry this man), to the time she made that statement to me. I then extrapolated from her statement that her sex life was one of the reasons (if not) the main one that caused her divorce. We must do our best to speak of the past, convey it, and remember it, in such a way that all lovers feel it is their responsibility to make sure mistakes done by others in their love lives—are not repeated. What is important is to change people's attitude toward love and marriage! How could a pretty girl be 'persuaded' to marry a man she would otherwise not marry? Is it not only in a corrupt patriarchal world that young and innocent girls would be 'persuaded' by even their mothers to marry men who are incompatible? A word for this *marabout* and his like: "Have you forgotten of what Islam requires of you as loving husbands"? Remember it is not enough just to feed and clothe your wives, thinking of yourselves as men of "special virtues". It is this type of attitude that make some women (who desire marriage) to rather spend their lives like birds on tree branches—and not wanting to tie themselves down to a family.

My friend "Danladi" was to me an abnormal test-tube baby bred by forces of a corrupt patriarchal world in their romantic laboratories. I met Danladi in Damascus, Syria, in the mid-80s. He was an economic migrant "coming out Africa"—a continent famously described in French as *le Continent qui pleure* (the weeping continent). I do disagree with this portrayal of Africa. After all, there are so many smiling faces on that beautiful continent. Moreover, every continent has got its own share of problems—both natural and man-made. But I must also admit that Africa's problems are so far the most over-whelming. Like other Africans in the mid-80s, Danladi had a very hard time surviving in the socio-economic climate prevailing then in Syria, because he spoke little Arabic. Worst of all, he and others like him had overstayed their visas. At that time, it was customary for African migrants to meet at a particular location during week-ends to discuss Africa and also their plight in a foreign land. Danladi's home was one of the preferred places where Africans got together to discuss their common woes. Here Africans talked about how they left Africa—some recounted terrifying tales of atrocities that contributed to their coming out of that continent. Some agreed that Africa's anemic economy was to blame. Others disagreed. Most of them seemed to blame some African leaders who ate themselves silly; dieted constantly with the nectar of power, and enjoyed every second of it. Everyone complained about the bizarre confluence of widespread poverty, political instability and preventable diseases on the continent. However, there were other aspects of our conversations that we never agreed with one another—love and romance.

Danladi for instance was an unrepentant proponent of the idea of living together before marriage. He believed that playing house for a few weeks or months (and even years) with someone he wants to marry was not only appropriate, but also justified. He believed in the "try it before I buy it notion". He was the leader of that "majority camp". This writer was alternatively the leader of the "minority camp" that believed in marriage before sex. The "minority camp's" argument was that; true lovers do not need log fires to keep them warm (not even in winter); they believed that, whenever there was true love, marriage acted as a "log fire" that kept romantic relationships even warmer. The "majority camp" led by Danladi would reject any woman they slept with and did not like. Danladi in particular did not give a damn about the looks of a particular woman, or for that matter her disposition. He was only interested in the (excuse me), "sweetness of the pudding". To him, the "sweetness of the pudding" was the best determinant in choosing a wife. Let's pause for a moment. Was the environment in Syria at that time conducive for Danladi to put theory to practice? Did he realize the realities on the ground? He did. He and his supporters knew Syria was not the place to try out their sexual adventures; they needed a more "friendlier and kinder" environment. He and members of his "camp" often complained of the *mam-nou-a*[16] environment in Syria. After all, this was a close–knit Islamic society that did not condone illicit sex. But they had a consolation in the fact that they were just there on "transit." and that as soon as they were able to save enough bucks they would quit for other destinations. For potential "political asylum" seekers, Germany was the most favorable destination; and for those wanting to make real cash, Japan was the country of choice. Going back to Africa was however not in the cards—unless of course one's "asylum" papers were rejected, or that one was denied entry into Japan.

Several years past, then I got the wind Danladi was in Taiwan. I tried to locate him and find out whether he had re-discovered the meaning of love and refashioned his old ideas about love and romance. I located him easily; he was then "shacking up" with a certain Filipino lady several years older than he was. To Danladi, his girl friend was never to be his wife, she was considered only as a "usable and expendable commodity". He surprisingly had not changed a bit since our days in Syria. He was still that happy and insouciant person I knew years

---

16.   Mam-nou-a' is an Arabic word that takes it's root from the verb *ma na a*; meaning 'to stop; to detain; to hinder; or to prevent'. When something is said to be mam-nou-a', it means it's forbidden; prohibited or inadmissible. Economic migrants, mostly Africans, used this word loosely to denote the 'inaccessibility of illicit sex" in their 'new country'.

back. He was good company; and did not burden me with worries and problems. He walked through life with enviable insouciance. This writer eventually came to the conclusion that, trying to make him understand the meaning of true love was only a gamble. Indeed, it was as uncertain as "throwing your wallet into a crowded street and hoping your wife would catch it!" This Filipino lady had been lured away by the bright lights of fake love. It was only after Danladi left her for another destination; this time Japan; did she realize she had lost the battle for his heart. Guilt and pain then became terrible exchanges for this Filipino lady, for she had allowed herself to be lured away by the bright lights of fake love. She had good reasons to feel crestfallen. It was not long before she packed up and left for her home town in the Philippines. In a male-dominated world, and in a world of romantic relationships; dreams and deception are likely to continue to occupy the stage for a long time to come.

CONCLUSION

The inter-relationship between love and sex was tackled in the first chapter of this book. Where love exists, should sex necessarily be an indispensable concomitant? Where sexual intercourse has taken place, does it mean it has only occurred because the two "consenting individuals" are in love? The natural bond that exists between love and sex, man and woman was discussed. The distortion of this bond through various means was also dealt with. It was also stated that having sex with one's spouse is a form of worship from the Islamic viewpoint. Some consequences associated with a freewheeling macho-attitude toward sex, were also discussed.

The meaning of love was dealt with in the second chapter. In this chapter, some general assumptions about what love is, was discussed. Some aspects of these assumptions were questioned. By defining love from an Islamic perspective, lovers were then categorized into two basic categories—true and fake lovers. It was argued that love is said to be defective if it does not end in marriage. In the third chapter, discussion was based on the sources of love. If everything has it's source, then where is the source of every love? Then again, from an Islamic perspective, love was said to have originated from God. Our knowledge of God was said to have been derived from the Prophets sent to mankind by Him—the last of them being Muhammad (p.b.u.h.) the Prophet of Islam. The authenticity of the *Holy Qur'an* held in reverence, and recited daily during their five daily prayers by the 1.3 billion Muslims around the world was ascertained. The credibility of the Prophet Muhammad as the Messenger of God was also discussed. But are true lovers only Muslims, Christians or Jews; what of Hindus, Buddhists, or those who believe in ancestor-worship, the worship of wood and metal; or simply believe in nothing? An anecdote was given to illustrate this point.

In the fourth part, a discussion on climbing the proverbial Mountain of Love by all lovers was centered on how best to get prepared before scaling this Mountain. The safest passage to follow, from an Islamic viewpoint, in climbing the Mountain was also discussed. Possible dangers to be encountered up the Mountain of Love were also highlighted. Then in the fifth chapter, a discussion on the attitude of lovers on top of the Love Mountain was made. It centered on marriage preparations that included the payment of *Mahr* or marriage gift and the size of the "wedding cake". Who and who should be invited to partake of the "wedding cake"? The rich and famous or just everybody particularly the poor?

The writer suggested the United Nations set up a UN High Commission for True Lovers (UNHC-TL). This Commission could be headed by the Secretary-General, Kofi Annan of Ghana; or by Madeleine Albright, former US Secretary of State. Under this Commission, some Eminent Statesmen who are considered true lovers could carry the UN Message of True Love to youngsters (and even old folks) around the world. In a nutshell, Sex Education; which is now being preached across the global village could be dropped and replaced with Love Education. The question is how do we indulge in sexual activities, when we have yet to understand love? It is up to the world to decide: Love first or Sex first. Love first means marriage before sex: If sex precedes marriage, then that could be said to be a milder form of rape! This writer thinks.

In the sixth part a discussion on who gets *what*, *how* and *when* in a romantic relationship was made. This was referred to by this author as the *diplomacy of love*. The argument was that: if lovers have been able to climb up to the top of the Love Mountain, what should they do in order to create good times for themselves; and keep the good times rolling? In *the diplomacy of love*, we find answers to these questions. Divorce was considered by the writer to be an old solution to marital problems. The writer could not have done justice to this book by failing to mention the sorry state of love affairs in a corrupt patriarchal world and it's attendant consequences.

The last part of this book addresses this phenomenon. In a corrupt and male-dominated world, the "World of Sex" belongs to the man. He uses and disposes of women as he wishes. Women almost always are at the short end of the love stick. Any one used to watching *Discovery Channel's* programs entitled: *The FBI Files; Medical Detectives;* or *Case Studies in Forensic Science* would realize that some aspects of these programs often show how some women, with misplaced loyalties often pay the price of being raped and killed by men of moral turpitude—men who sometimes use love as a means to rape and kill their victims. This writer is nervous about the state of love in about say half a century from now. That is about the year 2054.

In the year 1993 in Nashville, in the U.S., more than 1000 teen-agers; both boys and girls, wore white ribbons to signify virginity. These teen-agers went to Washington D.C. to attend a convention and re-affirm their dedication to chastity. The girls wore gold wedding bands that were given to them by their parents at a ceremony celebrating the promise not to have sex until they marry. The gold rings were to be given to their husbands on the wedding night. These teen-agers believed NO sex is the way to go. More than 200,000 other teens signed pledge cards stating they would not have sex until they marry. So nice! This group of teens is the torch bearer of True Love!

The writer's prayer:

> "O Lord! Let not our hearts deviate
> Now after Thou hast guided us,
> But grant us mercy from Thee:
> For Thou art the Grantor
> Of bounties without measure."[1]

---

1.   Qur'an, 3:8.

SELECTED BIBLIOGRAPHY

Allen, E. A. *History of Civilization.* Vol. 3.Cincinnati: General Publishing House,1889.

Allen, John L. *Student Atlas of World Politics.* Guilford Dushkin/McGraw-Hill, 1998.

Ali, Muhammad Mohar. *Sirat al–Nabi And The Orientalists.* 1ˢᵗ ed. Madina: King Fahd Complex for the Printing of The Holy Qur'an and Center for the Service of the Sunna and Sirah, 1997.

Ba'albaki, Munir. Al-Mawrid: *A Modern English-Arabic Dictionary.* Beirut:Dar el-elm Lil-Malayen, 1998

Badawi, A. Jamal. *The Status of Woman in Islam.* Plainfield: The Department of Education and Training, MSA of U.S. and Canada, 1980.

Baker, Robin. *Sperm Wars: The Science of Sex.* New York: Basic Books, 1996.

Al-Balali, Ahmad Hameed. Mal Maani' Minal Hijaab? Translated by Wael.F.Tabba'. Dammam: Dar Al-Thakhair, 1995.

Conferences On Muslim Doctrine And Human Rights In Islam: Between Saudi. Canonists and Eminent European Jurists, Second Conference of Paris. 2 November 1974. Riyadh: Ministry of Justice, and Beirut: Dar Al Kitaab Allubnani. n.d.

Conway, Jill. K. and Susan Carolyn Bourque. eds. *The Politics of Women's Education: Perspectives from Asia, Africa and Latin America.* Women and Culture. Ann Arbor: University of Michigan Press, 1993.

The Encyclopedia Britannica. 11ᵗʰ ed. Vol. 12. Cambridge: University Press, 1911.

The Hadiths

    i) *Al–Bukari* (died. 870 A.D.)

    ii) *Muslim* (died. 875 A.D.)

    iii) *Ibn Majah* (died.887 A.D.)

    iv) *Abu-Da'ud* (died. 888 A.D.)

    v) *Al-Timidhi* (died. 892 A.D.)

    vi) *Al-Nasa'i* (died. 915 A.D.)

Hadiths or Traditions of the Prophet: Most of the quoted *Hadiths* were translated from Arabic by the author. Quotations of these traditions have been chiefly based on the six most authentic sources; that were compiled in the latter part of the third century of Islam. And, although, a generation of *muhaddithun* (compilers of the traditions), compiled a huge corpus of *hadiths* during the succeeding centuries, twelve of such have been the most important. Out of these, six have gained such general approval that later generations tacitly accepted them as the Six Authentic Collections *(Sehah-al-Sittah)* as stated above.

Hart, Michael H. *The 100: A Ranking of the Most Influential Persons in History.* New York: Hart Publishing Company, Inc. 1978.

Masri, Ghalib, and Nazif *The Way To Happiness.* Riyadh. The Cooperative Council for Call and Guidance under supervision of the Presidency for Islamic Research, Ifta and Propagation, n.d.

Michener, James A. Islam: "The Misunderstood Religion." Readers Digest.(American Edition), May 1955, pp 68-70.

Nicolson, Harold "The Old and New Diplomacy." in *Politics and the International System.* ed. Robert L. Pfalzgaffz. 2nd ed. Philadelphia:Lippincot, 1972.

Qanbas, Abdul Halim Muhammad. *Al-Hubb Fil- Islam.* Damascus: Dar-al-Hikmah, 1977.

The Holy Qur'an: Translation of verses is heavily based on Abdullah Yusuf Ali's Translation. *The Holy Qur'an: English translations of the meanings and Com-*

mentary. Rev.and ed. The Presidency of Islamic Research, IFTA, Call And Guidance. Madina: King Fahd Holy Qur'an.Printing Press, 1983

Rocky Mountain News. "Would You Rather Be A Virgin? More Women Say Yes." *Woman's Own,* December 1994, 21.

Sabiq, al-Sayyid. *Fiqh Al-Sunnah.* Vol.2. Beirut: Dar-al Fikr, 1983.

Schur, Norman. *1000 Most Important Words.* New York: Ballantine Books,1982.

NEWSPAPERS

China Post (Taipei). 28 June 1989; 31 March 1993; 11 June 1995; 27 August, 30 November 1999; 16 March; 9, 23 April; 7 May; 28 September 2004.

Taiwan News (Taipei). 16 March 2004.

0-595-32886-5

Manufactured by Amazon.ca
Bolton, ON

46151215R00072